T0156766

SITUATION BASEBALL

BASEBALL

BASICS OF KNOWING WHAT TO DO WITH THE BALL

STEVE GELFIUS

authorHOUSE

AuthorHouse™
1663 Liberty Drive
Bloomington, IN 47403
www.authorhouse.com
Phone: 833-262-8899

Published by AuthorHouse 02/01/2024

ISBN: 978-1-4772-8509-1 (sc)
ISBN: 978-1-4772-8508-4 (e)

Library of Congress Control Number: 2012920478

Print information available on the last page.

Any people depicted in stock imagery provided by Getty Images are models,
and such images are being used for illustrative purposes only.
Certain stock imagery © Getty Images.

This book is printed on acid-free paper.

To our four athletic grand children for their interest to the continuing improvement and love for the game of BASEBALL, and to young ball players for their effort in keeping the game fun.

CONTENTS

INTRODUCTION

You've seen it many times. There are runners on base, the young ballplayer fields the ball and is confused as to where to throw it. Does he try to tag a runner out, a teammate says to throw to second base, a coach yells "throw home" and with the added confusion, what needed to be a pre- thought decision turns into no out and one more run for the other team. This booklet will get the ball players to concentrate on one question BEFORE the ball is hit and that is "what do I do if the ball is hit to me?". And a second part answers the question "where do I go if the ball is NOT hit to me?".

After the development of the physical skills of the game like fielding ground balls and fly balls, batting and running, the most fundamental area is the "smarts" of the game. Developing this skill can mean being a starter or a sub, it can give a player the edge of difference, it is the little things that make the big difference. This book gives infielders and outfielders the basic solutions to very base running situation. It gives situations that make them think to develop that instinctive sense of what to do with the ball. This book can be used in the field by coaches, in the backyard by dads, between players on the way to the game to build confidence. It is a basic tool for every player.

A couple of general assumptions should be stated. Unless identified, all balls hit to a player are ground balls. Obviously, the ball player needs training for plays that are in motion more than doubling up a runner. The answers on some situations can be the same as others. Circumstances can be quite variable for each situation, but we chose most common occurrences. In your training you may want to add a feature to see if it changes the answer, like "what if the ball had been hit to your right instead of your left". We have also tried to be gender neutral, but in a sport dominated by males please pardon our references to "he". And finally, some answers can be judgmental, but in all cases we go with the answer that makes the most sense for fundamental baseball at this level. In baseball one fundamental rule is to "play the percentages". There are twenty one situations for each infielder. They all start with a man on first with no outs and work their way up from there. With no one on base it's obvious that the only place to throw the ball is first base.

How to Read the Illustrations

✖ x's are base runners

● circles are the fielders

⟶ solid arrow indicates where the throw should go

┈┈▶ a dashed arrow indicates where a second-choice throw should go

RUN▶ solid arrow with the word "run" means to run with the ball to the base

LOOK▶ dashed arrow with the word "look" means to look that runner back to the bag before throwing

FIRST BASE SITUATIONS

The unique question for the first baseman is does he go to another base first with the throw before getting the possible easy out at first base first. The first baseman is responsible for the area between the first base line to one third of the way to second base. It is the only infield position that is most suitable for a left handed player. This position also requires not only the ability to field ground balls off the bat, but the throws from fellow infielders that are low and in the dirt. On throws from right field to home plate, he will serve as cut off man in the infield.

You are the first baseman. There is a runner on 1st and there are no outs. The ball is grounded to you. Where do you throw the ball?

Answer: Cut the lead runner down by going to 2nd where your shortstop should be covering. It is always more important to keep a runner out of scoring position if at all possible.

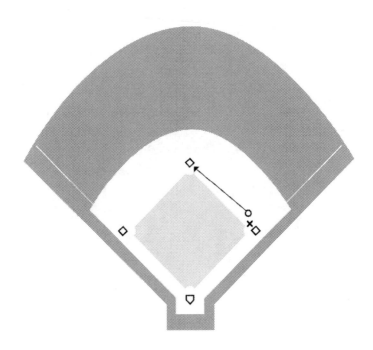

You are the first baseman. There is a runner on 1ˢᵗ and there is one out. The ball is grounded to you. Where do you throw the ball?

Answer: Cut the lead runner down by going to 2ⁿᵈ where your shortstop should be covering.

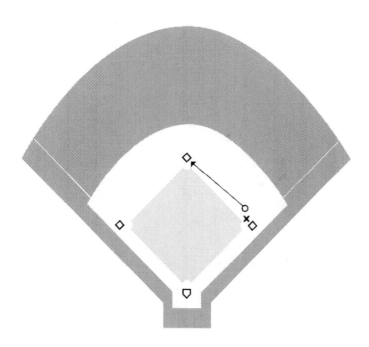

1st – 3

You are the first baseman. There is a runner on 1st and there are two outs. The ball is grounded to you. What should you do?

Answer: To avoid a possible throwing error, step on 1st to end the inning or give an under handed toss to your pitcher who should head to 1st on anything hit to his left side.

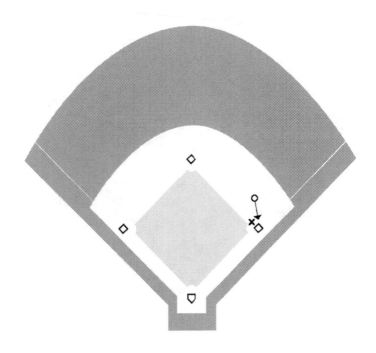

1st – 4

You are the first baseman. There is a runner on 2nd and there are no outs. The ball is grounded to you. What should you do?

Answer: Look the runner back to 2nd and go to 1st in person or toss to your pitcher coming towards 1st. If the 2nd base runner breaks for 3rd then throw to 3rd. Getting the lead runner out leaves you with one out and a runner on 1st instead of 2nd setting up a possible double play.

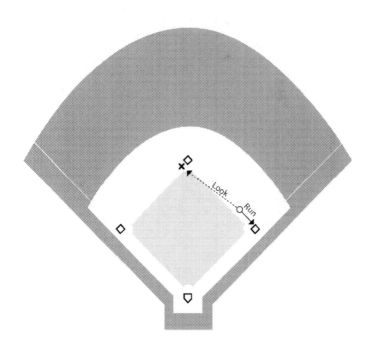

1st – 5

You are the first baseman. There is a runner on 2nd and there is one out. The runner on 2nd breaks for 3rd on a hard hit grounder that you field right at 1st base. What should you do?

Answer: Step on 1st and then throw to 3rd. If the runner is more than two thirds to 3rd you should hold your throw because you now have two outs and an errant throw lets the runner score.

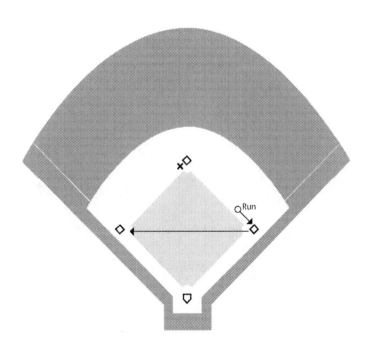

You are the first baseman. There is a runner on 2nd and there are two outs. You are playing at medium depth and a high chopper is hit to you. You determine you cannot get to 1st before the runner does. What should you do?

Answer: Toss to your pitcher who should be heading for 1st. On ALL balls hit to the 1st base side of the infield, it is the pitcher's responsibility to ALWAYS head for 1st for the cover.

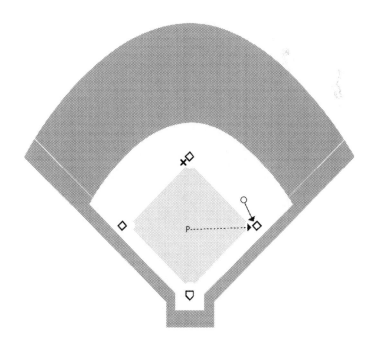

You are the first baseman. There is a runner on 3ʳᵈ and there are no outs. The score is tied and it's the middle of the game. You field a grounder to your right. Where do you go with the ball?

Answer: The 3ʳᵈ base runner will probably break for home. First choice is to cut the run down. If the runner does not break or you don't have a clear throw (pitcher coming to cover 1ˢᵗ may be in the way), then toss to your pitcher covering 1ˢᵗ.

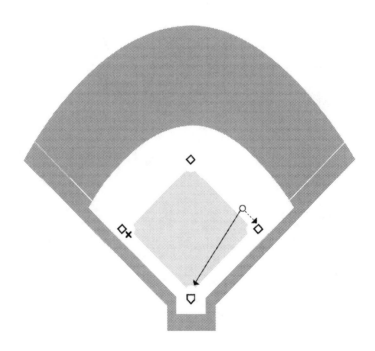

You are the first baseman. There is a runner on 3rd and there is one out. The game is tied, but it's only the second inning. A sharp grounder is hit straight to you. Where do you go with the ball?

Answer: You may have a chance to get the runner going home. If not, go to first. Although it is always good to prevent a run, another out makes it two outs and you still have plenty of game left. If the runner at 3rd hesitates, you can run to 1st as you keep an eye on the 3rd base runner.

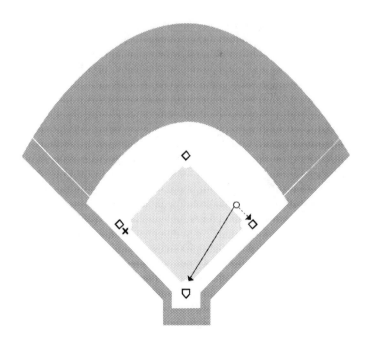

You are the 1st baseman. There is a runner on 3rd and there are two outs. A slow hopper is hit toward you allowing you to charge the ball causing your momentum to go toward home where the runner from 3rd is going. Where do you get the easiest out?

Answer: Throw to 1st where your 2nd baseman should be covering. This avoids any possible close call at home plate or the catcher having the ball knocked out of his glove.

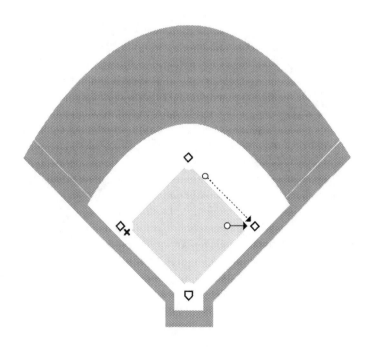

You are the first baseman. There are runners on 1st and 2nd and no outs. You are in the middle innings and your team is down by two runs. The ball is grounded to you. Where do you go with it?

Answer: Chances are you can't get the runner at 3rd so throw to 2nd where your shortstop should go to cover and he can then try for a double play by throwing back to 1st covered by you, your pitcher, or your second baseman. Getting at least one out and possibly two with a 2nd to 1st double play results in two outs and a runner at 3rd as apposed to no outs and bases loaded.

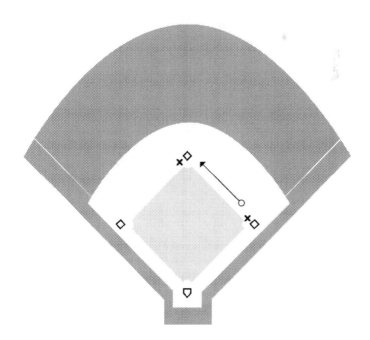

You are the first baseman. There are runners on 1st and 2nd and there is one out. The left handed batter hits a line drive to you. Where do you go with the ball?

Answer: You will want to double up one of the runners. Chances are you can get to 1st before that runner does but you'll have to look and make that decision very quickly.

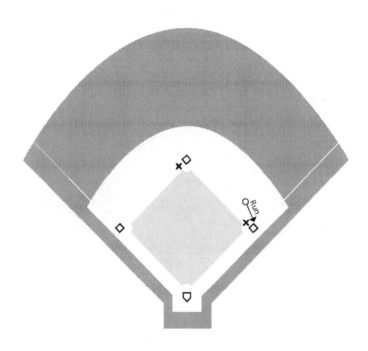

You are the first baseman. There are runners at 1st and 2nd and there are two outs. The ball is grounded to you. Where do you throw the ball?

Answer: Since all bases are a force out, go to the easiest which will be 1st base for you. If you can tag a bag instead of throwing, it eliminates any chance of an error.

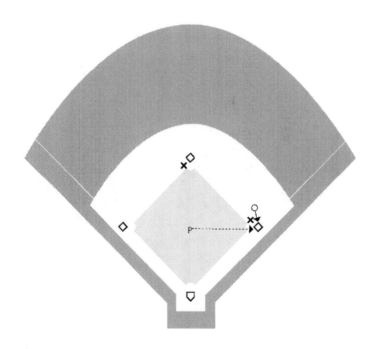

You are the first baseman. There are runners at 1st and 3rd and no outs. It is early in the game and the score is tied. What do you do with any ground ball hit to you?

Answer: Look the runner back to 3rd and throw to 2nd. If you try to get the 3rd base runner at home or 3rd and do not, you have still left a runner in scoring position on 2nd and there are still no outs. Throwing to 2nd allows a possible double play and you've got plenty of game left to get the run back.

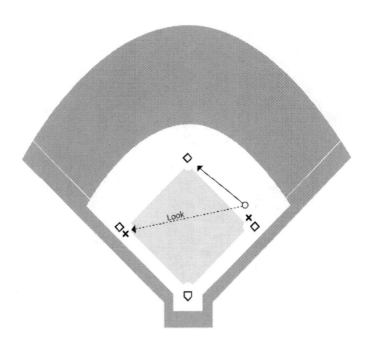

You are the first baseman. There are runners at 1st and 3rd and there's one out. It is late in the game and your team is down by one run. Your coach has the infield playing at regular depth. The ball is hit to you. Where do you throw?

Answer: Throw to 2nd for a double play. Looking the runner back to 3rd wastes time. He is heading home regardless and by looking him back (he doesn't have to run) you'll only have time to get one runner. 1st base will be covered by you or the pitcher.

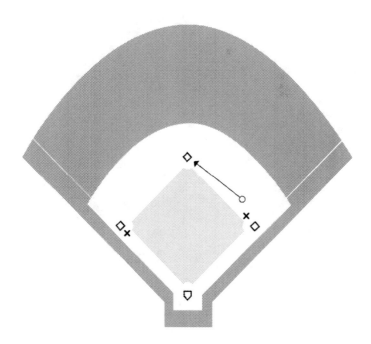

You are the first baseman. There are runners at 1st and 3rd and there are two outs. It is the top of the last inning and the score is tied. The ball is hit sharply to your right – you make a diving stop. Where do you go with the ball?

Answer: The force play to end the inning is either 1st or 2nd. Since you were forced right, 2nd base should be closer and your shortstop should be covering.

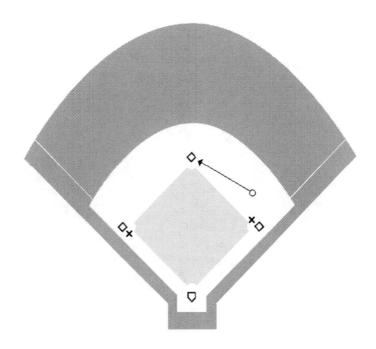

You are the first baseman. There are runners at 2nd and 3rd and there are no outs. The ball is grounded to you which you field cleanly. What should you do and where do you throw the ball?

Answer: Look the runner back to 3rd and you go to first, stepping on the bag or toss to the covering pitcher. If the 3rd base runner breaks for home, then throw home. This answer can change depending upon the number of runs you are ahead and what inning it is. But if you are behind, you need to prevent any more runs from scoring.

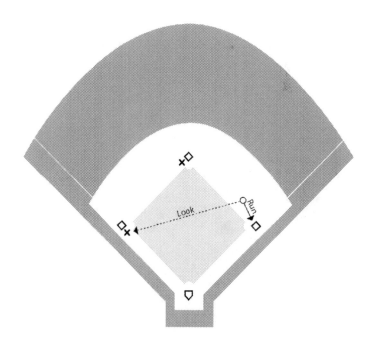

You are the first baseman. There are runners at 2nd and 3rd and there is one out. It is late in the game and your team is up by one run. You field a high hopper. Where do you throw the ball?

Answer: Given the situation, the other team will have the 3rd base runner going on any ground ball. You should throw home. Preventing a tying run late in the game is absolutely necessary. If you do not get the runner at home, the game is tied with still one out and yet another runner at 3rd.

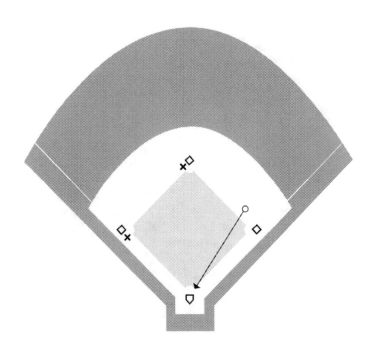

You are the first baseman. There are runners at 2nd and 3rd and there are two outs. Where do you throw any ground ball hit to you?

Answer: No matter how you field the ball, the easiest out will be at 1st base. In this situation the only runner any infielder should be concerned with is the batter going to 1st. When there are two outs, the only choice is the closest force out base.

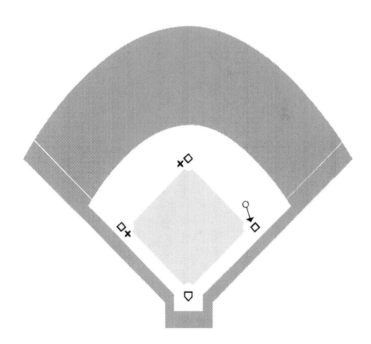

You are the first baseman. The bases are loaded and there are no outs. It is the middle innings and your team is down by two runs. The ball is grounded to you half way between 1st and 2nd. What should you do?

Answer: Throw to home and give your catcher a chance at a double play by throwing back to you or your pitcher at first. You really can't allow more runs to score when it is an easy force play at home.

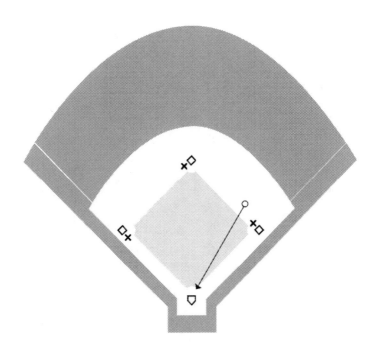

You are the first baseman. The bases are loaded and there is one out. It is late in the game and your team is ahead by three runs. The ball is grounded to you. Where do you throw the ball?

Answer: No matter the run spread, you should throw to home forcing the runner and not allowing another run. There is no risky tag when there is a force play at home plate and it allows your catcher who can see the entire field a chance at a double play by throwing back to 1st base.

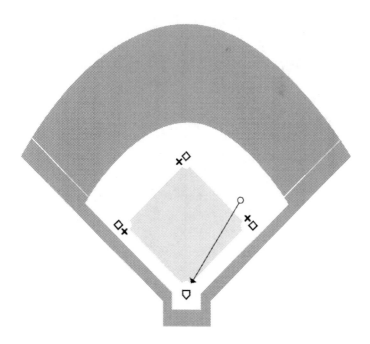

You are the first baseman. The bases are loaded and there are two outs. It is the bottom of the last inning and your team is up by one run. You are at medium play depth and the ball is hit as a sharp grounder to you. What should you do?

Answer: All bases are force outs to end the game so go for the easiest throw – either to 2nd or a run to 1st or toss to your pitcher heading for 1st base.

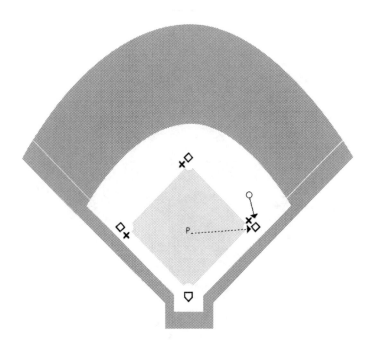

SECOND BASE SITUATIONS

The second baseman is pivotal to a team's success. Relied upon to cover first base on bunts and second base on steals, they need to be quick on their feet. They also have to be in good communication with their shortstop as to who is taking the throw to second from an outfielder or catcher. Strong throwing arms aren't as necessary as agility. They are responsible for the area from second base to two thirds the distance towards first base. A second baseman serves as cut off man for throws from right field to second or third and from right center field to second base.

2nd – 1

You are the second baseman. There is a runner on 1st and there are no outs. The ball is grounded to you toward your left. Where do you throw the ball?

Answer: Turn and throw to 2nd where your shortstop should be covering. Although it would be easier to toss the ball to your 1st baseman, your first choice is to cut down the lead runner to keep him out of scoring position on 2nd base.

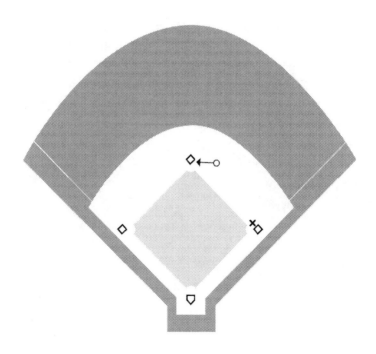

2nd – 2

You are the second baseman. There is a runner on 1st and there is one out. The ball is hit to you but to your left causing you to move toward 1st base to field the ball. Where should you throw the ball?

Answer: Although it would be easier with your momentum to go to 1st base, you should turn and throw to 2nd to cut down the runner that would then be in scoring position.

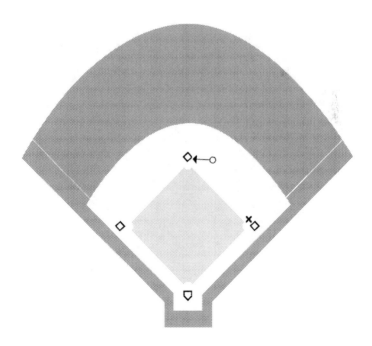

You are the second baseman. There is a runner on 1st and there are two outs. You field a sharply hit grounder. Which base do you throw to?

Answer: It's your choice of 1st or 2nd whichever you determine is the easiest throw. It will depend on which direction you go to field the ball. Most coaches will have you go to first since it is a more routine throw.

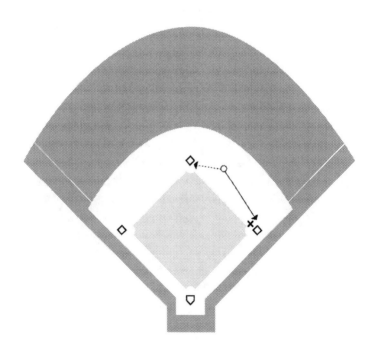

You are the second baseman. There is a runner on 2nd and there are no outs. The ball is hit to you. What should you do?

Answer: Chances are the 2nd base runner will break for third on any ground ball to the right side. If he does not, you can look him back and go to 1st with your throw. This decision really changes with how fast the ball gets to you, which direction you went to field it, did the runner have a lead off, will your 3rd baseman be in a position to take the throw, and what inning are you in and the run spread.

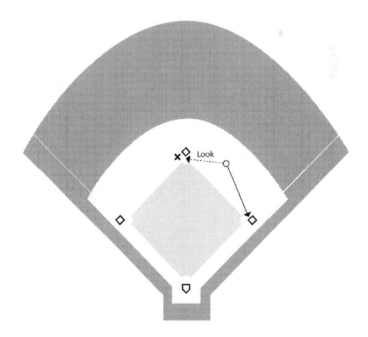

You are the second baseman. There is a runner on 2nd and there is one out. The ball is grounded to your right – very close to 2nd. Where do you go with your throw?

Answer: Chances are the 2nd base runner will break for third on any ground ball to the right side. If you feel you can get the runner at third, your momentum is in your favor, otherwise, you should throw to 1st. As in the previous situation, this choice depends on several factors.

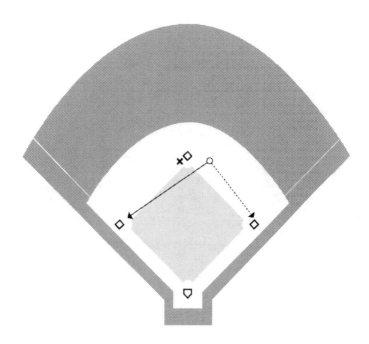

You are the second baseman. There is a runner on 2nd and there are two outs. Where do you go with any ground ball hit to you?

Answer: This is an easy one. Always go to 1st to get you out of the inning. Remember this, when there are two outs and no force play except 1st base, then 1st base is the ONLY choice.

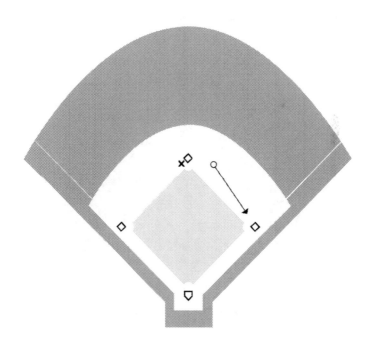

You are the second baseman. There is a runner on 3rd and there are no outs. The score is tied and it's early in the game. The ball is hit up the middle right which you cut off. Where should you go with the ball?

Answer: Chances are you won't be able to get the runner at home, but look just in case, then turn and go to 1st. Your choice here is to have one out and nobody on base or no outs and a runner at 1st. Your play at the plate may allow the batter to go to 2nd and be in another scoring position.

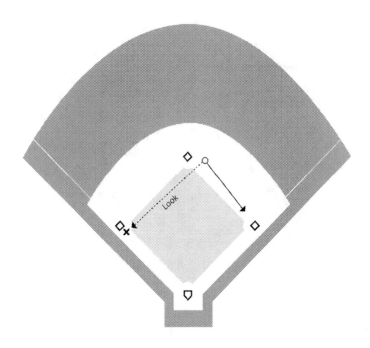

You are the second baseman. There is a runner on 3rd and there is one out. The game is tied, but it's only the second inning. A sharp grounder is hit straight to you. Where do you go with the ball?

Answer: You may have a chance to get the runner going home but only if it is a sure thing. Throw to 1st base giving you two outs in the inning and giving up the run and what could be a close call at home. Remember, it is early in the game and an errant throw or loose ball allows the batter to get to 2nd base.

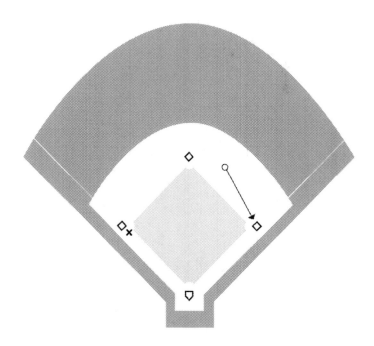

You are the second baseman. There is a runner on 3rd and there are two outs. A slow hopper is hit toward you allowing you to charge the ball causing your momentum to go toward home where the runner from third is going. Where do you get the easiest out?

Answer: Throw to 1st base. This avoids any possible close call at the plate or the catcher having the ball knocked out of his glove and it gets you out of the inning. A force out play is the easiest and in this situation 1st base is the only answer.

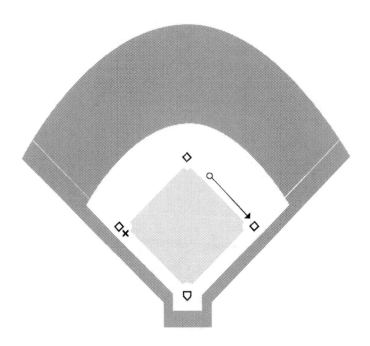

You are the second baseman. There are runners at 1st and 2nd and no outs. You're in the middle innings and your team is down by two runs. The ball is grounded to you. Where do you go with it?

Answer: Chances are you can't get the runner at 3rd, so throw to 2nd where your shortstop should be covering and he can then try for the double play by throwing to 1st.

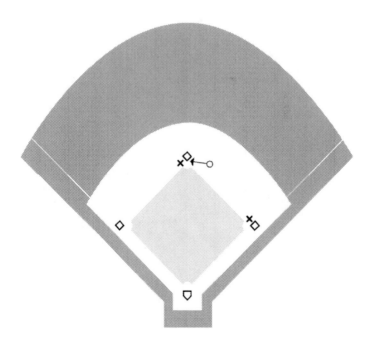

You are the second baseman. There are runners at 1st and 2nd and there's one out. The left handed batter hits a line drive to you. Where do you go with the ball?

Answer: Your shortstop should have been playing more toward second base with the left handed batter, so go to 2nd to try to double up the lead runner.

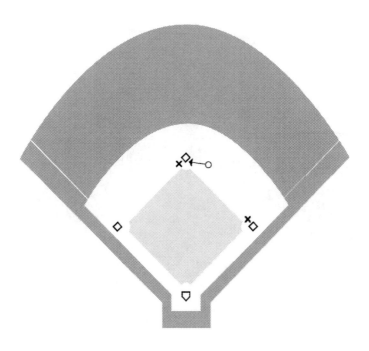

You are the second baseman. There are runners at 1st and 2nd and there are two outs. The ball is grounded to you. Where do you throw the ball?

Answer: Since all bags are a force out, go to the easiest which is probably 1st base. Throwing to 1st base is the most routine throw you have practiced. It will have the highest percentage of accuracy.

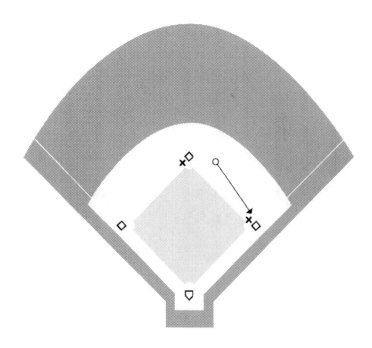

You are the second baseman. There are runners at 1st and 3rd and no outs. The ball is hit to you as a regular ground ball. It's early in the game and the score is tied. What do you do with the ball?

Answer: You should look the runner back at 3rd and throw to 2nd base. No more than a glance to 3rd because your objective here is a double play. Allowing a run to score early in the game for a possible two outs and for sure keeping a runner off 2nd base is a good trade.

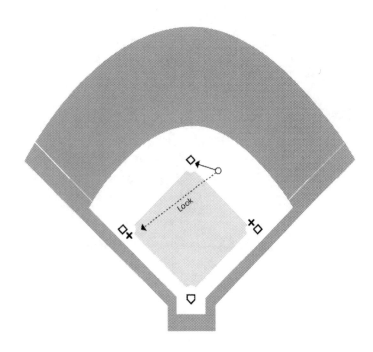

You are the second baseman. There are runners at 1st and 3rd and there is one out. It's late in the game and your team is down by one run. The ball is hit sharply to you. What should you do?

Answer: Throw to 2nd base where your shortstop is covering. A double play gets you out of the inning, so looking the runner back to third just wastes time. If you try to get the runner at 3rd and fail, you will be left with still one out and runners at 1st and 2nd base. If the double play attempt fails, you now have two outs with a runner on just 1st base.

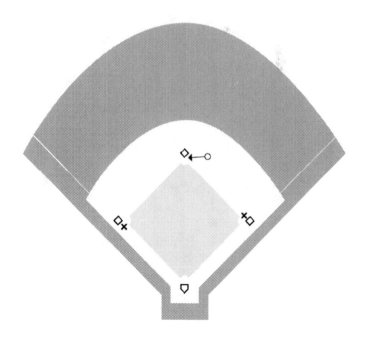

You are the second baseman. There are runners at 1st and 3rd and there are two outs. It's the top of the last inning and the score is tied. The ball is hit sharply to your right – you make a diving stop. Where do you go with the ball?

Answer: The force play to end the inning is either 1st or 2nd. Since you were forced extremely right and you have to pick yourself up off the ground, a throw to 2nd base should be closer and an easy toss to your shortstop.

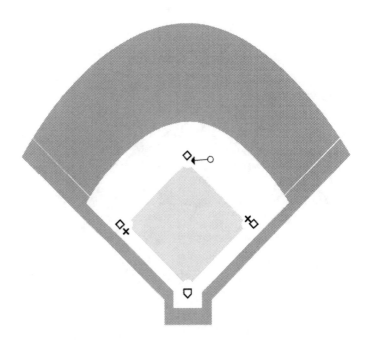

You are the second baseman. There are runners at 2nd and 3rd and there are no outs. The ball is hit to your left which you field cleanly. What should you do and where do you throw the ball?

Answer: Look the runner back to 3rd and throw to 1st. Getting the runner at 3rd base to hesitate will still leave you enough time to make the short throw to 1st base. If the 3rd base runner breaks for home – throw home. This decision may depend upon the inning you are in and the run spread. The result of getting the 3rd base runner out is that you have one out with runners at 1st and 2nd base setting up a force at any bag or a double play.

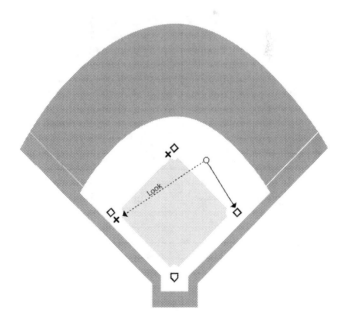

You are the second baseman. There are runners at 2nd and 3rd and there is one out. The ball is hit to you as a high hopper. What should you do and where do you throw the ball?

Answer: Look the runner back to 3rd and throw to 1st. Now you have two outs and have prevented a run from scoring, but if the 3rd base runner breaks for home, then throw home. If you do not get the out at home plate you will have the possible double play coming up with the next batter.

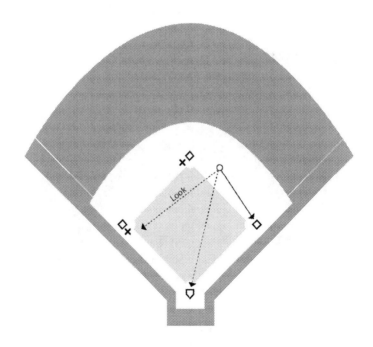

You are the second baseman. There are runners at 2nd and 3rd and there are two outs. The ball is hit to you. Where should you throw the ball?

Answer: No matter how you field the ball, the easiest out will be at 1st to get out of the inning. The only force out is at 1st base and a force out is easier than a tag out.

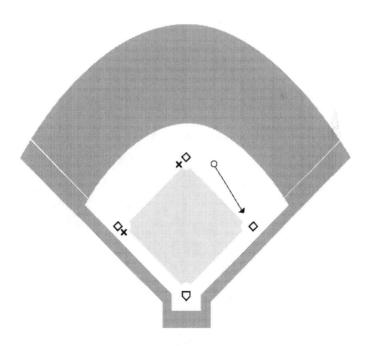

You are the second baseman. The bases are loaded and there are no outs. You are in the middle innings and your team is down by two runs. The ball is grounded to you half way between 1st and 2nd. What should you do?

Answer: Go home and give your catcher a chance at a double play by going to 1st. Any base here is a force out and you have a couple options for a double play, but preventing a run and getting at least one out is priority.

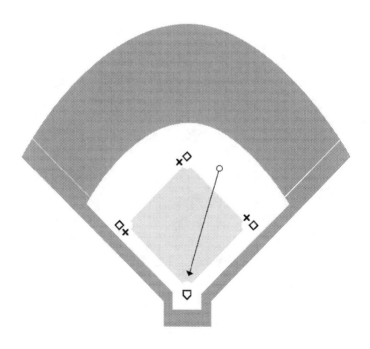

You are the second baseman. Bases are loaded and there is one out. It's late in the game and your team is ahead by three runs. The ball is grounded to you. Where do you throw the ball?

Answer: Throw to 2nd base letting your shortstop to try for the double play to end the inning. Since you are up by three runs, you can afford to give up a run if the double play attempt fails. This would leave you with two outs and a runner at 1st and 3rd base – still a safe situation to get the third out.

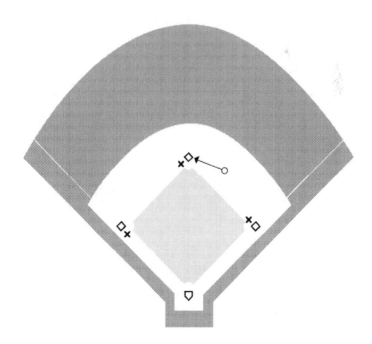

You are the second baseman. Bases are loaded and there are two outs. It's the bottom of the last inning and your team is up by one run. You are at medium play depth and the ball is hit as a sharp grounder to you. What should you do?

Answer: Throw to 1st base. This is your easiest out and easiest throw.

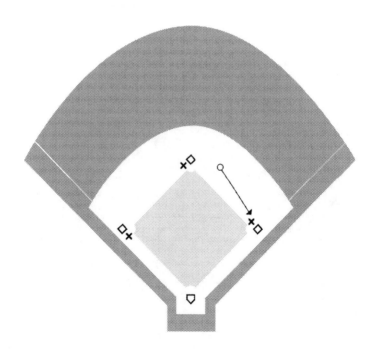

THIRD BASE SITUATIONS

In baseball third base is commonly called "the hot corner". Since most batters are right handed, the third baseman may share most of the ground balls with the shortstop. His responsible area covers from the third base line to a third of the way to second base. Most of the throws coming to him will be to tag out the runner. On throws from left field, he will serve as the cut off man in the infield.

You are the third baseman. There is a runner on 1st and there are no outs. There is a slow hopper hit to you that you have to move forward to field. Where do you throw the ball?

Answer: Your first choice is 2nd to keep the runner out of scoring position, but if the runner got a good jump towards 2nd and/or is a fast runner, then your safe choice is 1st base.

Helpful hint: before the pitch, determine the speed ability of the runner.

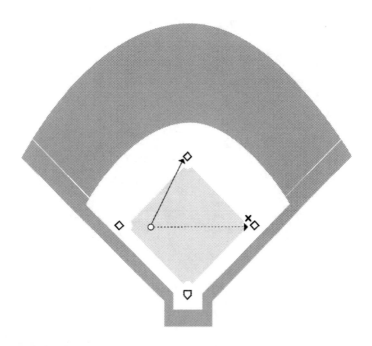

You are the third baseman. There is a runner on 1st and there is one out. The ball is hit sharply to you, but instead of fielding it cleanly, you knock the ball down and have to pick it up. Where do you throw the ball?

Answer: Your first choice is 2nd to keep the runner out of scoring position, but since you didn't field the ball cleanly, that may have given the runner enough time to get to 2nd safely. Look to 2nd base, make your determination and go to 1st base as your second choice. The important thing is to get one more out so that with two outs you can just concentrate on getting the next batter out.

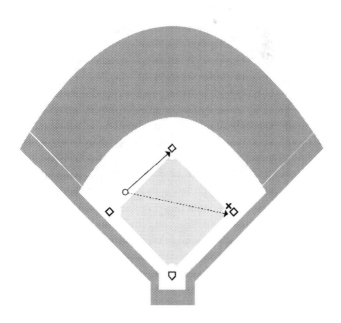

3rd – 3

You are the third baseman. There is a runner on 1st and there are two outs. The ball is hit to you. Where do you throw the ball?

Answer: Take your time and do the routine throw to 1st. This is what you practice the most and it avoids the possibility of your 2nd baseman getting to the bag late or a fast runner making the play at 2nd close.

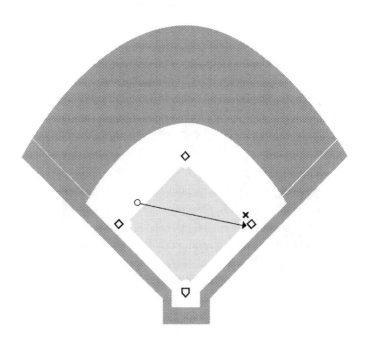

You are the third baseman. There is a runner on 2nd base and there are no outs. The ball is hit to you and you field it cleanly. What should you do?

Answer: You should look the runner back to 2nd and throw to 1st, but be sure to then head for 3rd to cover in case the 2nd base runner breaks for 3rd after you throw to 1st, although your shortstop should be heading for 3rd for such coverage.

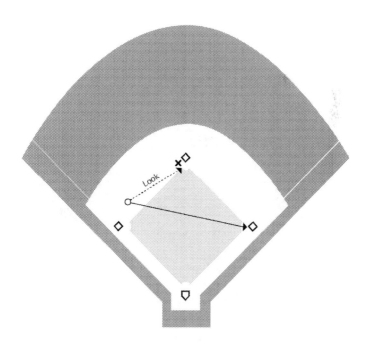

You are the third baseman. There is a runner on 2nd base and there is one out. It's late in the game and your team is up by five runs. The ball is hit to you. What should you do with it?

Answer: You should look the 2nd base runner back and throw to 1st. In the event the 2nd base runner has broken off the bag too far toward 3rd, your second baseman should be near second for a possible run down. Get back to 3rd for a possible throw back to you from your first baseman.

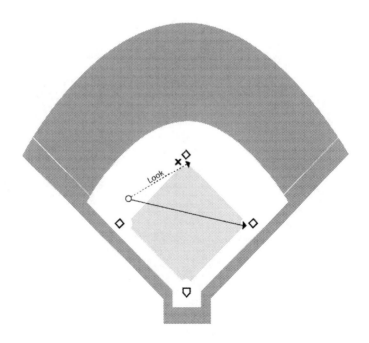

You are the 3rd baseman. There is a runner on 2nd base and there are two outs. The ball is hit to your left causing you to move toward the pitcher's mound to field it. Where do you throw the ball?

Answer: With two outs there's only one place to think about and that's 1st base.

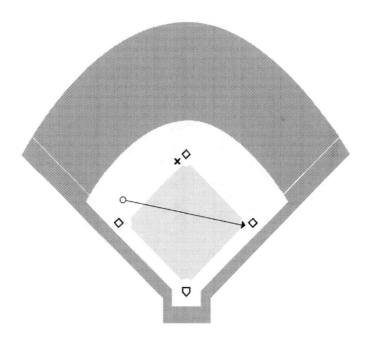

You are the third baseman. There is a runner on third and there are no outs. The ball is hit to you. The runner appears to bluff a break for home. What do you do?

Answer: Look the runner back to third. As soon as he moves in the direction of 3rd, you throw to 1st. If the runner breaks for home, you throw to the catcher. With no outs you would like to get the only runner in scoring position. This decision may depend on the inning you are in and the run spread. The important thing is to get an out.

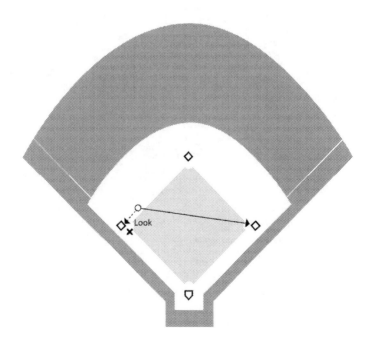

You are the third baseman. There is a runner on third and there is one out. It's early in the game and your team is ahead by two runs. The ball is hit sharply to you, which you have to knock down and pick the ball up with your bare hand. Where do you throw it?

Answer: If the runner breaks for home, throw to the plate if you are sure to get the out. Otherwise, you throw to 1st making it two outs and you're still up by one run early in the game. This is one of those situations that the coach should instruct his infield prior to the batter coming to the plate. That way it takes the pressure off the player's decision.

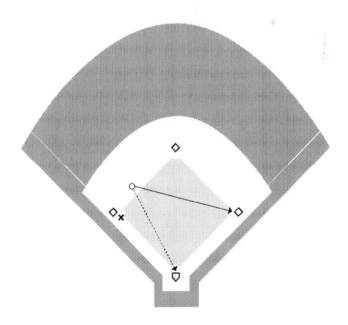

You are the third baseman. There is a runner on third and there are two outs. The ball is hit to you and the runner breaks for home. Where do you throw the ball?

Answer: With two outs you always take the easy throw to 1st base. It's the most routine throw you make and avoids a collision or close tag at the plate.

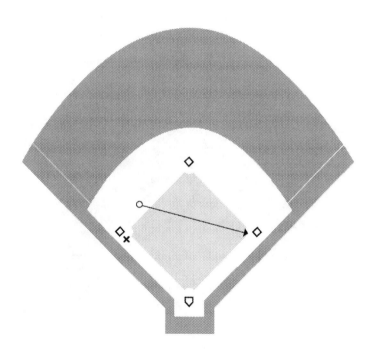

You are the third baseman. There are runners at 1st and 2nd and there are no outs. The ball is hit to you, but you have to go deep in the hole to your right to field it. What do you do now?

Answer: You should be able to run and tag 3rd base forcing the out, then decide to throw to 2nd or 1st for a double play. You may have more time to get the out with a throw to 1st base leaving you with two outs and only one runner on. Trying to get the runner at 2nd after tagging 3rd would be difficult, but you should glance.

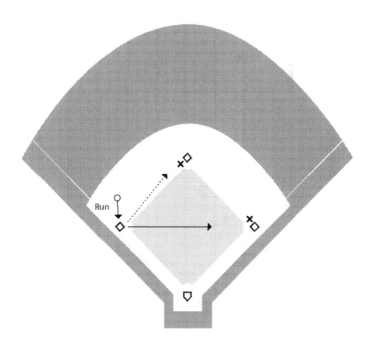

You are the third baseman. There are runners at 1st and 2nd and there is one out. The batter is a slow runner, but the 1st base runner looks pretty speedy. The ball is hit to you as a routine hopper. What are your options?

Answer: You have two double play options. First is the routine 2nd to 1st, but given the speed of the runners and one less throw, your best option is to tag the bag at 3rd and throw to 1st.

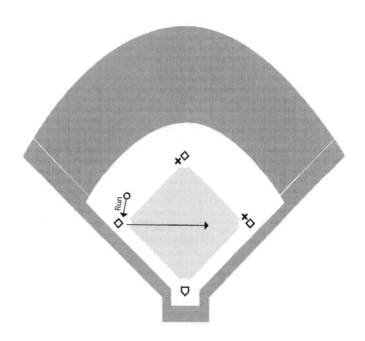

You are the third baseman. There are runners at 1st and 2nd and there are two outs. A really slow grounder is hit to you forcing you to come in on the ball. Where do you throw the ball?

Answer: Although your shortstop goes to third to cover the bag, you must remember that when there are two outs, your primary concern is the batter. So throw to 1st base to end the inning.

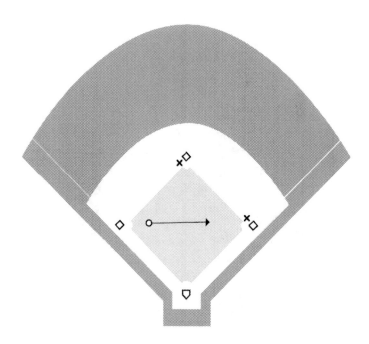

You are the third baseman. There are runners at 1st and 3rd and there are no outs. The ball is hit to you as a regular ground ball. It's early in the game and the score is tied. What do you do?

Answer: You should look the runner back to third and throw to 2nd, but you'll need to hurry. If you spend more than two seconds looking the runner back, you'll need to go to 1st. Remember that a batter has a little further to run (especially a right handed batter) to 1st base than the runner going from 1st to 2nd. First the batter has the extra step across the plate, and second, when he hits the ball the resulting swing slows his momentum in starting for 1st. Whereas the 1st base runner either has a lead off or is set to run as soon as the ball is struck.

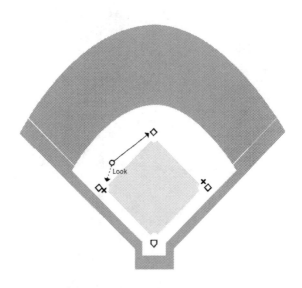

You are the third baseman. There are runners at 1st and 3rd and there is one out. It's late in the game and your team is down by one run. The ball is hit sharply to you. What should you do?

Answer: Your team really can not afford to give up another run at this point in the game. Look the 3rd base runner back to 3rd and throw to 2nd base. By keeping the runner at 3rd and getting the out at 2nd, you now have the same runner situation as before, but now there are two outs with a force at 1st or 2nd to end the inning.

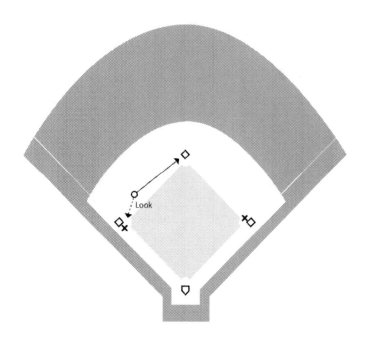

You are the third baseman. There are runners at 1st and 3rd and there are two outs. It's the top of the last inning and the score is tied. The ball is hit down the 3rd baseline but you make a diving stop. Where do you throw the ball?

Answer: The force play is at 2nd or 1st. Go to whichever will be the easiest throw to make to insure you get the runner – chances are it will be 1st base because it takes the average runner longer to get to 1st than to 2nd.

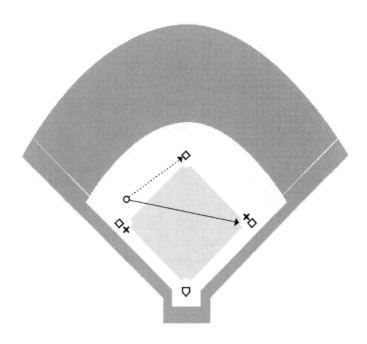

You are the third baseman. There are runners at 2nd and 3rd and there are no outs. The ball is hit to your left which you field cleanly. What should you do and where do you throw the ball?

Answer: A runner on 3rd can score so easily if there is any hesitation from an infielder. Since there are no outs the other team may be aggressive in their base running and have the 3rd base runner going on any ground ball. Look the 3rd base runner back to 3rd and throw to 1st, but if he is going home, then throw to the plate. Whether you get him out or not at the plate, you will be left with runners at 1st and 3rd.

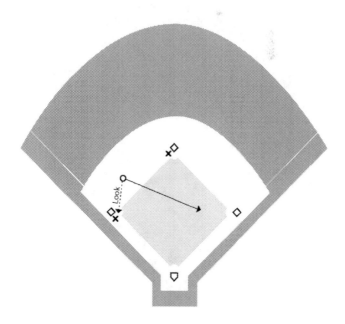

You are the third baseman. There are runners at 2nd and 3rd and there is one out. The ball is hit to you as a high hopper. What should you do and where do you throw the ball?

Answer: This is the same answer if there are no outs and depends upon the run spread and the inning. Basically, look the runner back to 3rd and throw to 1st. If the 3rd base runner breaks for home, then you should throw to home to prevent the run.

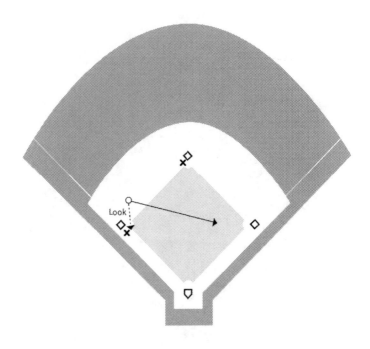

You are the third baseman. There are runners at 2nd and 3rd and there are two outs. The ball is hit to you. Where should you throw the ball?

Answer: There are two outs and only one base is a force out, so throw to 1st base for the easiest out and the most routine throw to get you out of the inning.

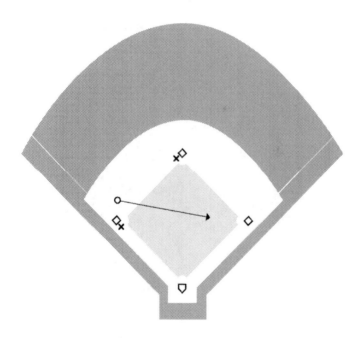

You are the third baseman. Bases are loaded and there are no outs. You're in the middle innings and your team is down by two runs. The ball is hit to you. What should you do?

Answer: If you are close enough to third base, touch the base and then throw to home for the catcher to tag the runner. Otherwise, throw to home and let the catcher have the force play and he then decides where to throw for the second out which will probably be first, but be ready because he could throw it right back to you for the force at 3rd.

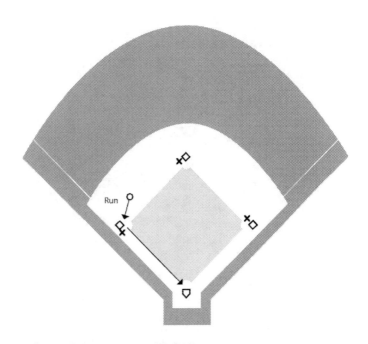

You are the third baseman. Bases are loaded and there is one out. It's late in the game and your team is ahead by five runs. The ball is hit to you. Where do you throw the ball?

Answer: No matter the run spread, you should throw to home forcing the runner and not allowing another run. You should then cover third in case the catcher decides to force the runner at third for the third out.

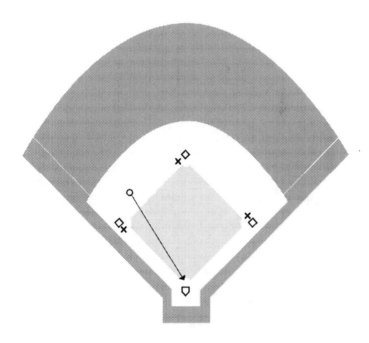

You are the third baseman. Bases are loaded and there are two outs. It's the bottom of the last inning and your team is up by one run. You are at medium play depth and the ball is hit as a sharp grounder to you. What should you do?

Answer: Run and tag third base to end the game. Always go for the nearest force play and particularly one where the ball doesn't leave your hand.

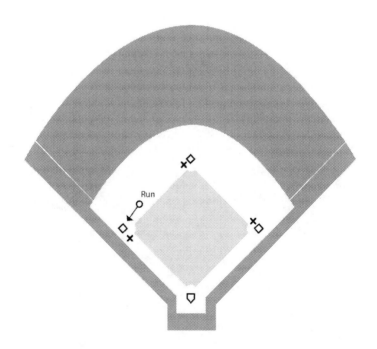

SHORTSTOP SITUATIONS

The shortstop is usually the fastest and best fielding player on the team. He is responsible for the area deep in the hole behind third base over to second base. He is the cut off man for throws to third base form center and left field and to second base from left and left center fielders. On most throws to first base it is further for the shortstop than it is for the third baseman.

SS – 1

You are the shortstop. There is a runner on 1st and there are no outs. The ball is grounded to you toward your left. Where do you throw the ball?

Answer: Throw to 2nd or if you're close enough, tag the bag. With your momentum carrying you toward 2nd, you might be able to beat the runner and not have to hit your second baseman with a perfect throw.

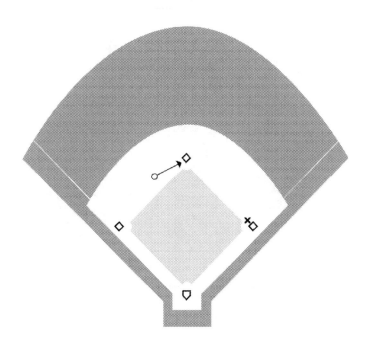

You are the shortstop. There is a runner on 1st and there is one out. The ball is hit to you but to your right. Your 3rd baseman tells you to go to 1st. Where should you throw the ball?

Answer: You should look to 2nd to see if your 2nd baseman is covering and if so, throw there to cut down the lead runner and keep him out of scoring position. 1st base is your second choice if the 1st base runner was going to beat the throw or your second baseman was not in a position to take the throw. An out is worth trading for a base runner.

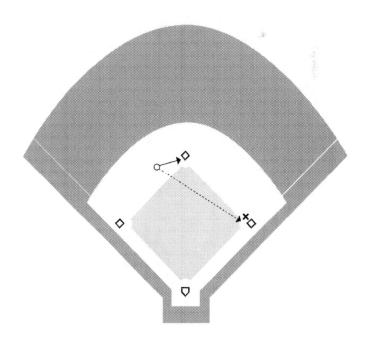

You are the shortstop. There is a runner on 1ˢᵗ and there are two outs. You field a sharply hit grounder. Which base do you throw to?

Answer: It's a force play at either 2ⁿᵈ or 1ˢᵗ base to end the inning. Go to whichever is easiest, probably depending upon how close to 2ⁿᵈ base you or your 2ⁿᵈ baseman is, but many times the routine throw to first is the easiest.

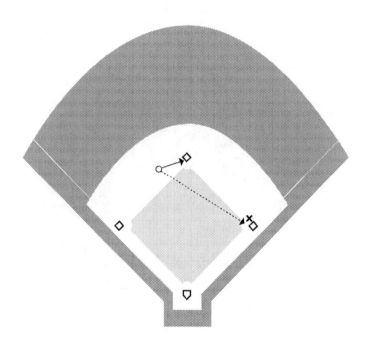

You are the shortstop. There is a runner on 2nd and there are no outs. The ball is grounded to you. What should you do?

Answer: The runner will not break for 3rd since you have the ball and could easily tag or throw him out, but look him back to 2nd anyhow and throw to 1st base.

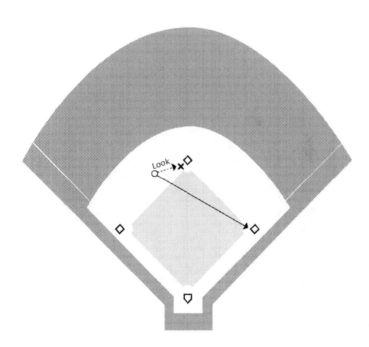

You are the shortstop. There is a runner on 2nd and there is one out. The ball is grounded to your right so much so, the 3rd baseman moves to his left diving for the ball. The 2nd base runner's first instinct was to hold but sees that 3rd is open and runs for it. What should you do?

Answer: Since your momentum is towards 3rd and if you're not too deep, you can probably tag the runner if not get him into a run down if he starts back to 2nd. If you are well ahead in the game, let the runner go and throw to 1st for the second out.

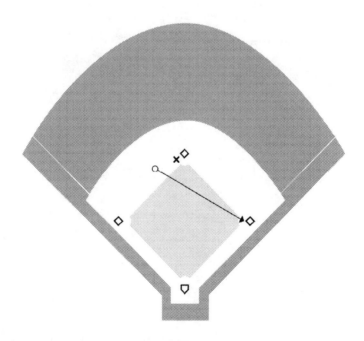

You are the shortstop. There is a runner on 2ⁿᵈ and there are two outs. Where do you go with any ground ball hit to you?

Answer: Always go to 1ˢᵗ to end the inning.

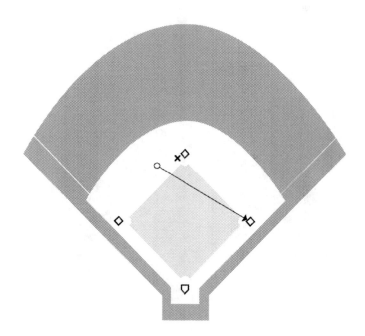

You are the shortstop. There is a runner on 3rd and there are no outs. The score is tied and it's early in the game. The ball is hit up the middle which you cut off. Where should you throw the ball?

Answer: Chances are you won't be able to get the runner at home who will be running on any grounder, but look just in case (like he could stumble), then throw to 1st base.

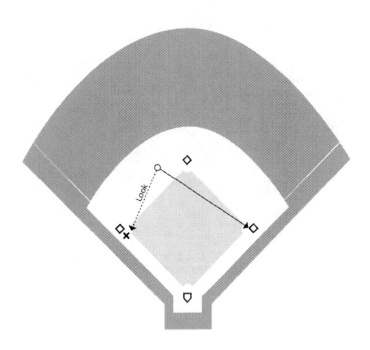

You are the shortstop. There is a runner on 3rd and there is one out. The game is tied but it is only the second inning. A sharp grounder is hit straight to you. Where do you go with the ball?

Answer: You may have a chance to get the runner going home and if you are sure then throw to the plate. If you are not completely sure, you still have time to throw to 1st base to get the second out and it is still early in the game.

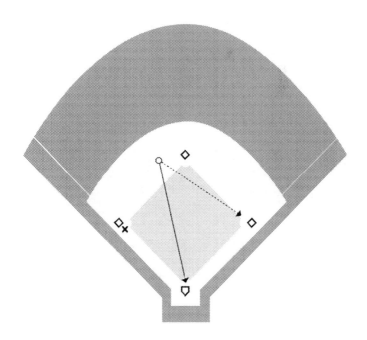

You are the shortstop. There is a runner on 3rd and there are two outs. A slow hopper is hit toward you allowing you to charge the ball and forcing your momentum to go toward home where the runner from 3rd is going. Where do you get the easiest out?

Answer: Throw to 1st base. This avoids any possible close call or the catcher having the ball knocked out of his glove. It is a force out and a routine throw.

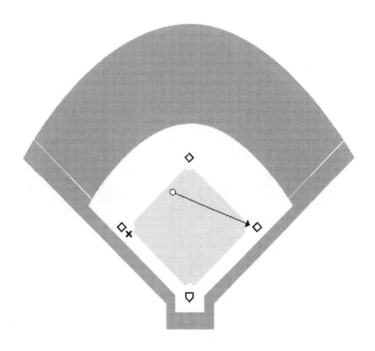

You are the shortstop. There are runners at 1st and 2nd and no outs. You're in the middle innings and your team is down by two runs. The ball is grounded to you. Where do you go with it?

Answer: You could go for a double play here, but you really don't want a runner at 3rd that could put you down another run. Go to third and let your 3rd baseman decide what other bag if any to throw to. If he elects not to relay the throw, you have the same situation with the next batter with the same possible double play to get out of the inning.

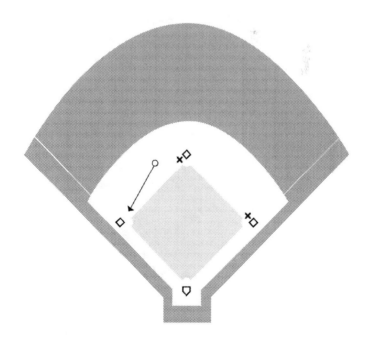

You are the shortstop. There are runners at 1st and 2nd and there is one out. It's the middle innings and the score is tied. The left handed batter grounds the ball to you, but you bobble the catch. Now what should you do?

Answer: You were probably planning on throwing to 2nd and then on to 1st for the double play to get you out of the inning, but since the throw to 1st will be late and you can only get one out, throw to 3rd to force the runner there because that is the lead runner.

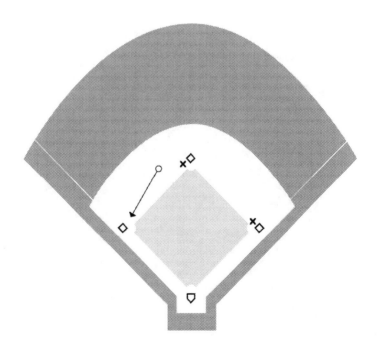

You are the shortstop. There are runners at 1st and 2nd and there are two outs. A very slow grounder is hit to you. Where should you throw the ball?

Answer: Since the two base runners may have a lead off or at least a good jump on a slow grounder, the batter has the furthest to run and a safe throw to 1st gets you out of the inning.

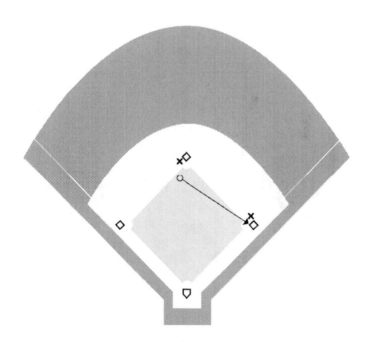

You are the shortstop. There are runners at 1st and 3rd and no outs. It's early in the game and your team is up by three runs. The ball is grounded to you and the runner at 3rd breaks for home. Where should you throw the ball?

Answer: Throw to 2nd to go for the double play. Since it's early in the game you can give up a run to get two thirds through the inning.

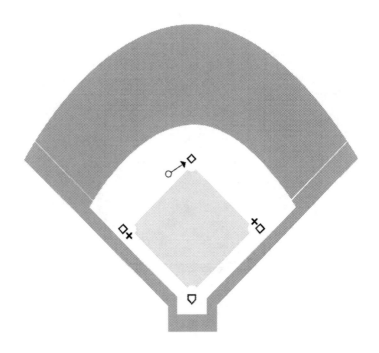

You are the shortstop. There are runners at 1st and 3rd and there is one out. It's late in the game and your team is down by one run. The ball is grounded sharply to you. What should you do?

Answer: Throw to 2nd. A double play gets you out of the inning, so looking the runner back to third just wastes time.

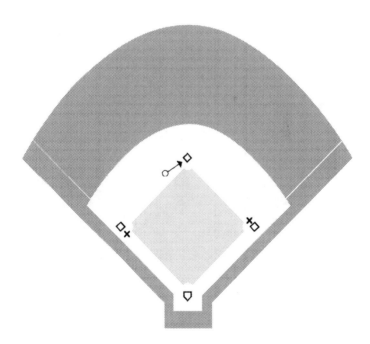

You are the shortstop. There are runners at 1st and 3rd and there are two outs. It's the top of the last inning and the score is tied. The ball is hit sharply to your right – you make a diving stop to knock the ball down. Where do you go with the ball?

Answer: The force play to end the inning is either 1st or 2nd. Chances are 1st base will be your easier out.

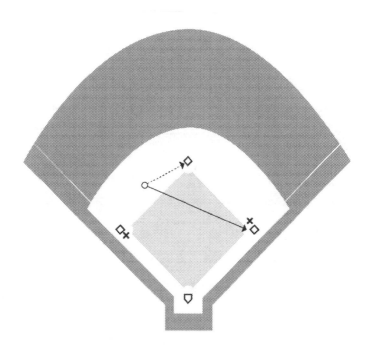

You are the shortstop. There are runners at 2nd and 3rd and there are no outs. It is in the middle innings and it looks like it could rain at any minute. The ball is grounded to your left which you field cleanly. What should you do and where do you throw the ball?

Answer: Look the runner back to 3rd and throw to 1st. If you are playing at any decent depth, it is doubtful you will be able to get the runner going home. This decision could change depending upon the score.

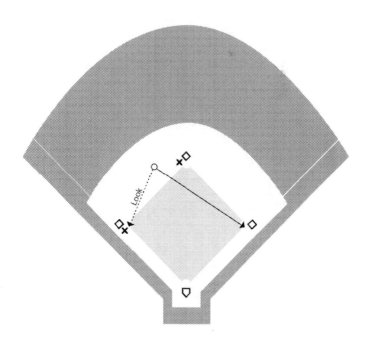

You are the shortstop. There are runners at 2nd and 3rd and there is one out. The ball is hit to you as a high hopper. What do you do and where do you throw the ball?

Answer: Look the runner back to 3rd and throw to 1st. Unless you are playing with the infield drawn in, you probably won't get the 3rd base runner if he has already decided to go home. At least you will have two down and only one runner on base.

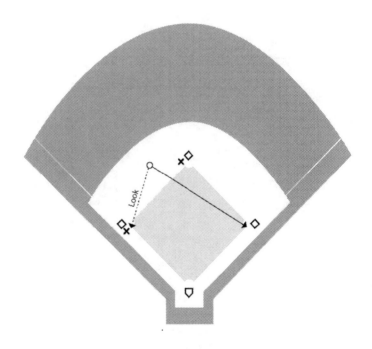

You are the shortstop. There are runners at 2nd and 3rd and there are two outs. The ball is grounded to you. Where should you throw the ball?

Answer: No matter how you field the ball, the easiest out will be at 1st to get you out of the inning.

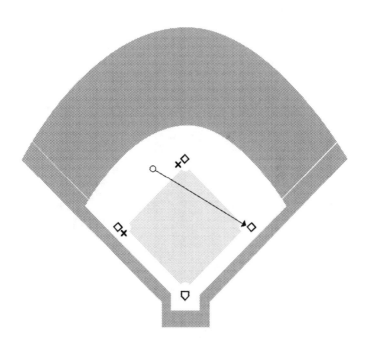

You are the shortstop. The bases are loaded and there are no outs. You are in the middle innings and your team is down by two runs. The ball is grounded to you. Where should you throw the ball?

Answer: Throw home for the easy force play that prevents a run and gives your catcher a chance at a double play with him then throwing to 1st base.

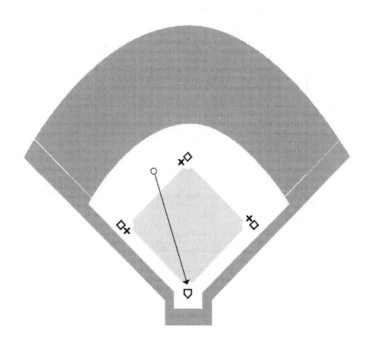

You are the shortstop. The bases are loaded and there is one out. It's late in the game and your team is ahead by three runs. The ball is grounded to you. Where do you throw the ball?

Answer: Since you are ahead by this much, you can take the chance on getting a double play to end the inning. The best combo will be the standard throw to 2nd and on to 1st. If the score was tied or it is even a one run spread either way, then you will probably be throwing home.

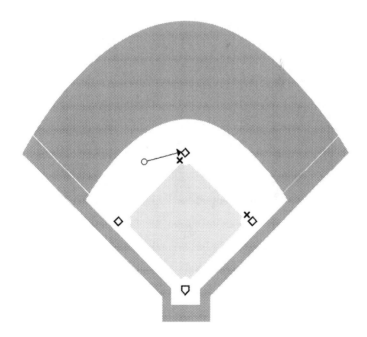

You are the shortstop. The bases are loaded and there are two outs. It's the bottom of the last inning and your team is up by one run. You are at medium play depth and the ball is hit as a sharp grounder to you. What should you do?

Answer: There is a force at any base to end the inning, so go with your easiest throw – probably the most routine one – a throw to 1st base.

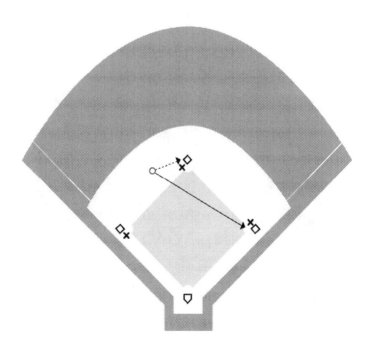

PITCHER SITUATIONS

The pitcher is also an infielder and can be overlooked when it comes to training on throwing situations. The pitcher will have the shortest throws to all the bases and being the most accurate thrower gives him priority on fielding bunts.

Pit – 1

You are the pitcher. There is a runner on 1st and there are no outs. A two hopper is hit right back to you. Where do you throw the ball?

Answer: Cut down your lead runner by throwing to 2nd – maybe allowing a double play.

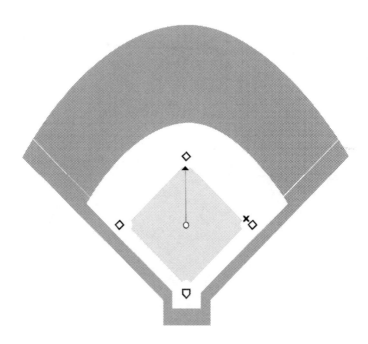

Pit – 2

You are the pitcher. There is a runner on 1st and there is one out. Where should you throw any ground ball you field?

Answer: Cut down the lead runner by going to 2nd base with your throw.

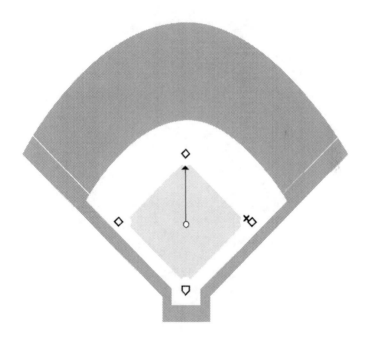

Pit – 3

You are the pitcher. There is a runner on 1st and there are two outs. Where should you throw any ground ball hit to you?

Answer: 1st base to end the inning.

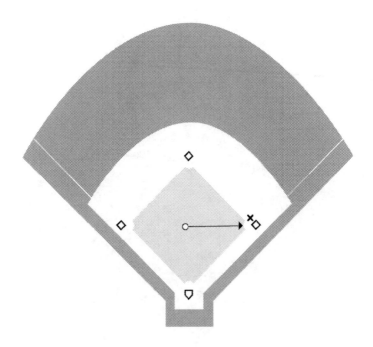

Pit – 4

You are the pitcher. There is a runner on 2nd and there are no outs. What should you do on any ground ball hit to you?

Answer: Look the runner back to 2nd and throw to 1st base.

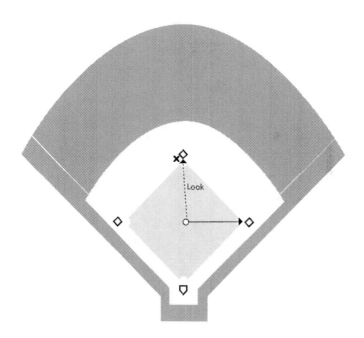

Pit – 5

You are the pitcher. There is a runner on 2nd and there is one out. What should you do on any ground ball hit back to you?

Answer: Look the runner back to 2nd and throw to 1st base.

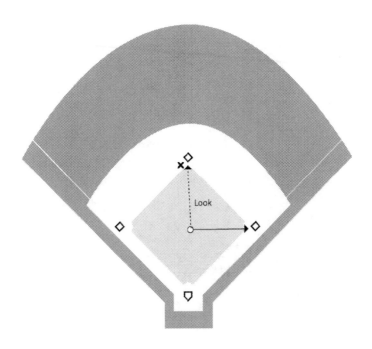

Pit – 6

You are the pitcher. There is a runner on 2nd and there are two outs. Where do you throw the ball on any grounder hit back to you?

Answer: Just throw to 1st to end the inning.

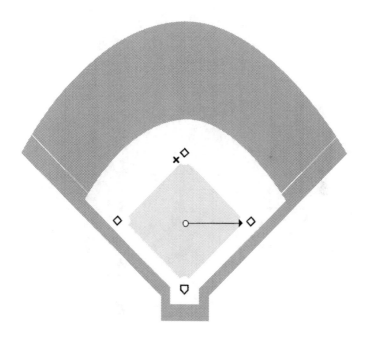

You are the pitcher. There is a runner on 3rd and no outs. It is late in the game and your team is ahead by one run. A little dribbler is grounded to the right side of the infield which you field cleanly. Where do you throw the ball?

Answer: Chances are the 3rd base runner is breaking for home. You should have time to throw home.

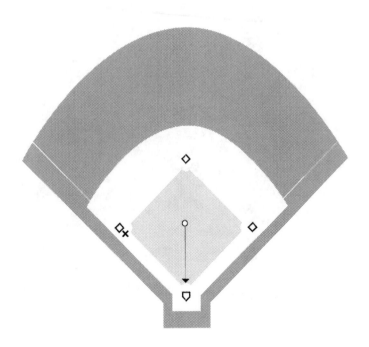

You are the pitcher. There is a runner on 3rd and there is one out. What should you do with any ground ball you field?

Answer: If the 3rd base runner breaks for home, then throw home. If not, look him back to third and throw to 1st base.

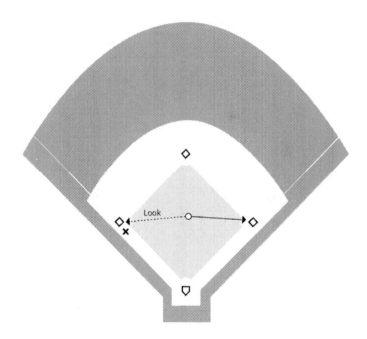

Pit – 9

You are the pitcher. There is a runner on 3rd and there are two outs. What do you do with any ground ball you field?

Answer: Throw to 1st for the easy force and end the inning.

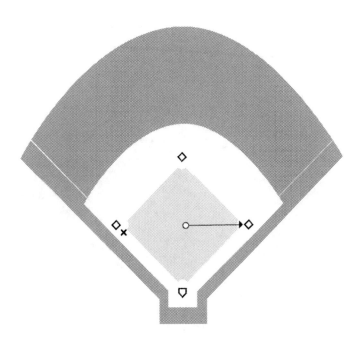

You are the pitcher. There are runners at 1st and 2nd and no outs. You are in the early innings and the score is tied. What should you do with any routine grounder?

Answer: Throw to 3rd to cut down the lead runner. Only if you were pulled drastically toward 1st and/or bobble the ball would you throw to 1st.

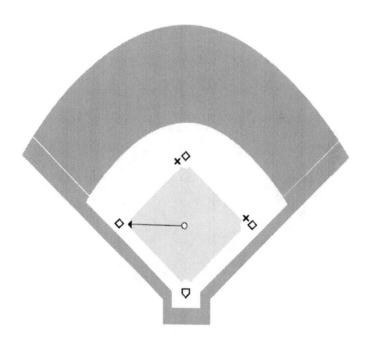

You are the pitcher. There are runners on 1st and 2nd and there is one out. What should you do with any routine grounder?

Answer: Throw to 3rd to cut down the lead run. The one exception would be a one hopper back to you on the mound where you can start a double play by going to 2nd. But any miscue allows the lead runner to score.

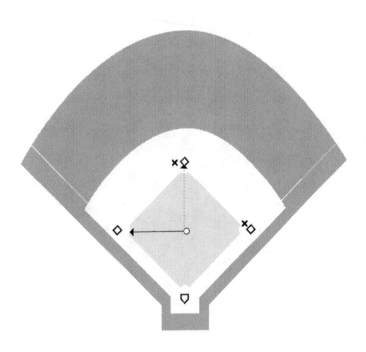

Pit – 12

You are the pitcher. There are runners on 1st and 2nd and there are two outs. It is late in the game and the score is tied. Where do you go with any ground ball?

Answer: Any ball to your right, throw to 3rd. Any ball to your left, throw to 1st. Most coaches will have you go to 1st regardless.

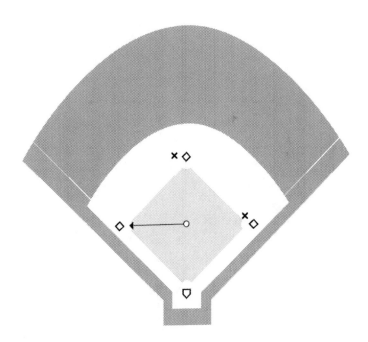

Pit – 13

You are the pitcher. There are runners at 1st and 3rd and there are no outs. What do you do with a ball grounded back to you?

Answer: Depending upon the score and how far you are into the game, you should look the runner back to 3rd and throw to 2nd.

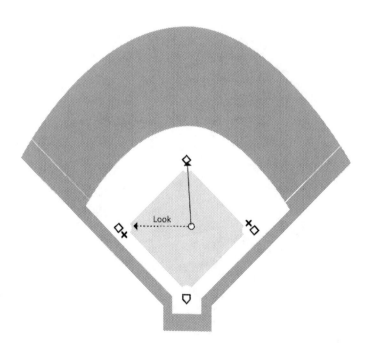

Pit – 14

You are the pitcher. There are runners at 1st and 3rd and there is one out. What do you do with a ball grounded back to you?

Answer: You should go for a double play by throwing to 2nd. To get this done you will not have time to look the runner back to 3rd.

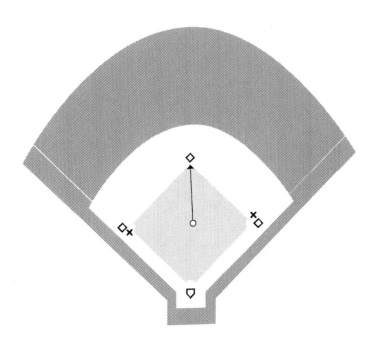

You are the pitcher. There are runners on 1st and 3rd and there are two outs. It is the top of the last inning and the score is tied. The ball is hit to your left – you make a diving stop. Where do you throw the ball?

Answer: The safest throw to end the inning will be to 1st base.

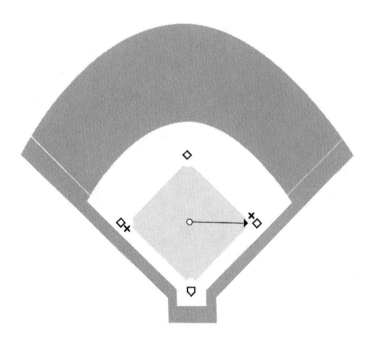

Pit – 16

You are the pitcher. There are runners at 2ⁿᵈ and 3ʳᵈ and there are no outs. What do you do with any ball grounded back to you?

Answer: Look the 3ʳᵈ base runner back and throw to 1ˢᵗ base.

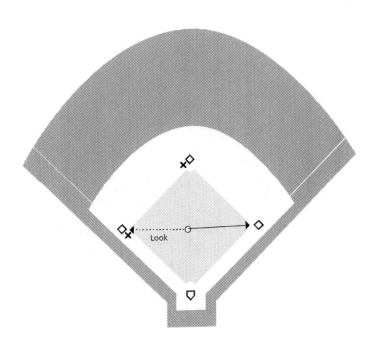

You are the pitcher. There are runners at 2nd and 3rd and there is one out. It is the bottom of the last inning and your team is up by one run. The batter is the number 8 hitter in the line up and he is a slow runner. A two hopper is hit back to you. What should you do?

Answer: Given these circumstances, throw to 2nd so your shortstop can make the double play to end the game.

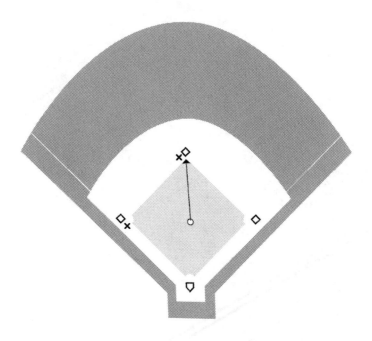

Pit – 18

You are the pitcher. There are runners at 2nd and 3rd and there are two outs. The left handed batter puts a bunt down the 3rd base line and he is a very fast runner. Where is the safest play?

Answer: Chances are the bunt play was on to score the runner from third. You probably will not get the runner going to 1st, so throw home. Even if the 3rd base runner does not go home, you still have prevented a run, leaving you with bases loaded and a force at all bases.

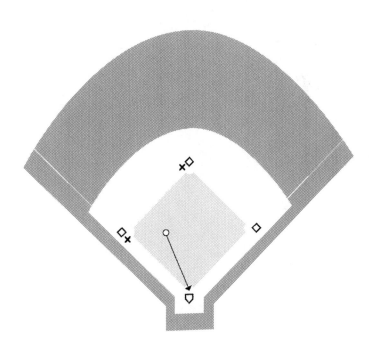

You are the pitcher. The bases are loaded and there are no outs. What do you do with any ground ball hit back to you?

Answer: Regardless of the score, throw home to prevent the run from scoring.

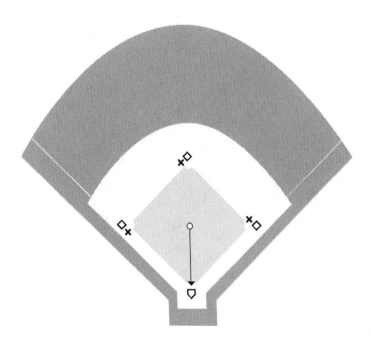

Pit − 20

You are the pitcher. The bases are loaded and there is one out. Where do you throw any ground ball that you field cleanly?

Answer: Throw home for the force play that prevents a score.

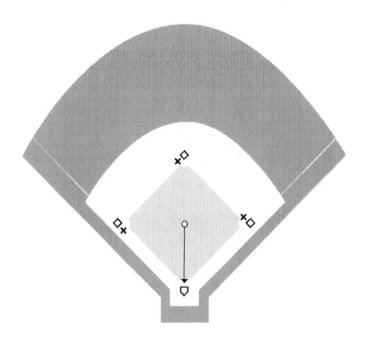

Pit – 21

You are the pitcher. The bases are loaded and there are two outs. Where should you throw any ground ball hit back to you?

Answer: All bases are a force out, but usually 1st base will be your best routine throw.

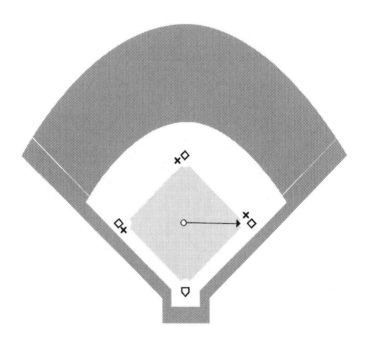

OUTFIELD SITUATIONS

For the outfield the throwing decisions can be repetitive given the number of outs. Routinely the outfielder is to throw to his cut-off man unless the two are so close that the outfielder can execute the throw the cut-off man would have done anyhow.

Since fly balls in the infield usually result in the runners holding their positions, those situations were not covered in the infield chapters. We've covered fly ball situations in this chapter since those base runner positions can change depending upon where the ball is thrown. In the following situations, the first example is for a ground ball and the second example (A) is for a caught fly ball.

You are the left fielder. There is a runner on 1st and there are no outs. A ground ball is hit to you. Where do you throw the ball?

Answer: As an outfielder you most generally throw to your cut-off man which in your case will be your shortstop. The runner on 1st will get to 2nd on a base hit. Your shortstop will come straight out or position him self between you and 3rd base. If you throw to 2nd, the runner can advance to 3rd on the throw. This solution also applies if there is one out or two outs.

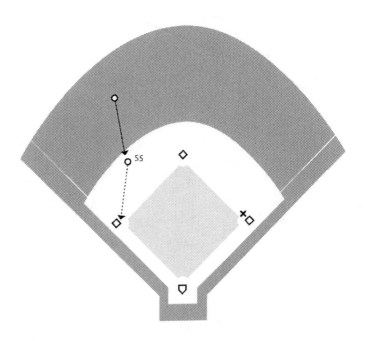

You are the left fielder. There is a runner on 1st and there are no outs. A fly ball is hit and caught by you. Where do you throw the ball?

Answer: Unlike a ground ball, the 1st base runner has the option of staying on 1st or tagging up and heading to 2nd. Your shortstop should now align him self between you and 2nd base. Throw to him. This solution also applies if there is one out.

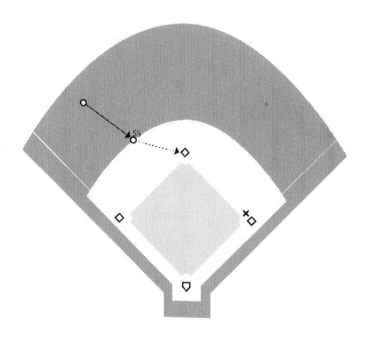

LF – 2

You are the left fielder. There is a runner on 2ⁿᵈ and no outs. A ground ball is hit to you. Where do you throw the ball?

Answer: The 2ⁿᵈ base runner will score on a hit so your concern is the new runner rounding 1ˢᵗ. Throw to your cut-off man who will then throw or move to cover 2ⁿᵈ base. This solution also applies if there is one out or two outs.

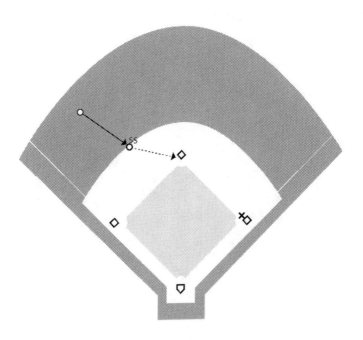

LF – 2A

You are the left fielder. There is a runner on 2nd and no outs. A fly ball is hit and caught by you. Where do you throw the ball?

Answer: The runner on 2nd can stay or tag up and head for 3rd. Your shortstop should position himself straight out from his position or between you and 3rd. Throw to your shortstop. If you throw to 2nd, the runner can head to 3rd. Do not throw behind the runner. This solution also applies if there is one out.

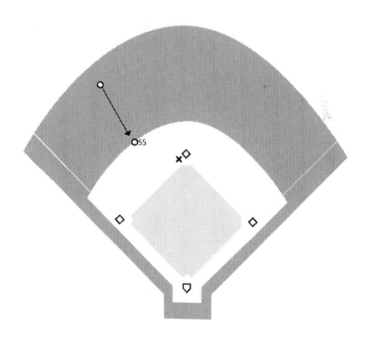

LF – 3

You are the left fielder. There is a runner on 3rd and no outs. A ground ball is hit to you. Where do you throw the ball?

Answer: Since the 3rd base runner will score on any base hit, your concern is the runner rounding 1st, so throw to your cut-off man who is the shortstop to keep the runner from coming to 2nd. This solution also applies if there is one out or two outs.

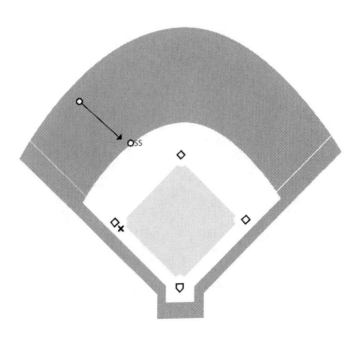

You are the left fielder. There are runners on 1st and 2nd and no outs. A ground ball is hit to you. Where do you throw the ball?

Answer: The 2nd base runner will probably score, so you need to be concerned with the runner coming to 2nd. Throw to your shortstop who should come straight out toward you or position himself between you and third base. This solution also applies if there is one out or two outs.

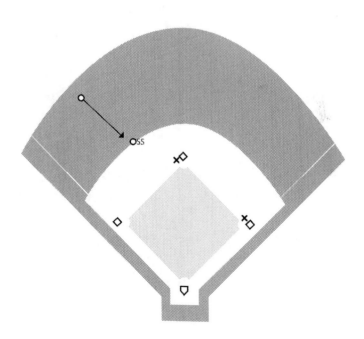

LF – 4A

You are the left fielder. There are runners on 1st and 2nd and no outs. A fly ball is hit and caught by you. Where do you throw the ball?

Answer: Since you want to keep the 2nd base runner from advancing to 3rd, you should throw to your cut-off man – the shortstop who should be between you and 3rd base. This solution also applies if there is one out.

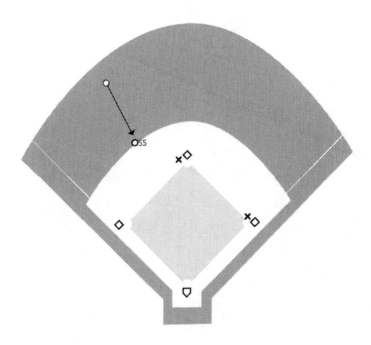

LF – 5

You are the left fielder. There are runners on 1st and
3rd and no outs. A ground ball is hit to you. Where do
you throw the ball?

Answer: This situation is the same as if you have a
runner on just 1st because the 3rd base runner scores on
a hit or a fly ball. So once again, throw to your shortstop
who is your cut-off man. He will then be responsible for
getting the ball to 2nd base. This solution also applies
if there is one out or two outs.

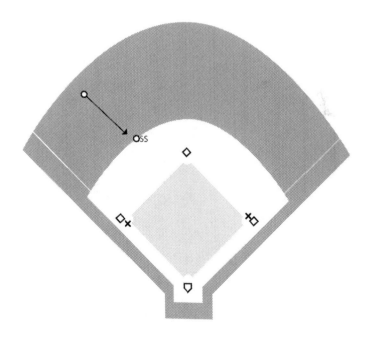

LF – 5A

You are the left fielder. There are runners on 1ˢᵗ and 3ʳᵈ and no outs. A fly ball is hit and caught by you. Where do you throw the ball?

Answer: Since the 3ʳᵈ base runner will tag up and score, your concern is the 1ˢᵗ base runner who does not have to run, but could tag up and go to 2ⁿᵈ. Once again throw to your shortstop who should be between you and 2ⁿᵈ base. This solution also applies if there is one out.

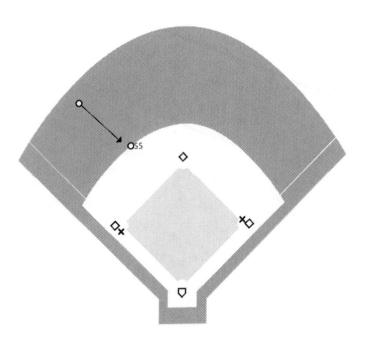

You are the left fielder. There are runners on 2nd and 3rd and there are no outs. The ball is grounded to you. Where do you throw the ball?

Answer: Since both runners will probably score on a base hit, your concern is the runner rounding 1st base. You need to keep him from going to 2nd, so throw to your cut-off man. This solution also applies if there is one out or two outs.

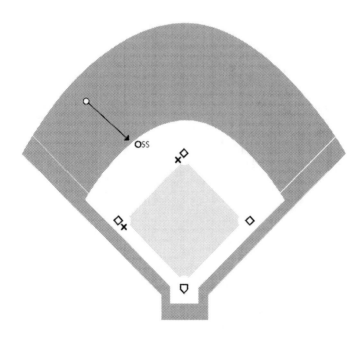

You are the left fielder. There are runners on 2nd and 3rd and there are no outs. A fly ball is hit and caught by you. Where do you throw the ball?

Answer: The runner on 3rd will tag up and score, but the 2nd base runner does not have to run. To keep him from advancing to 3rd, throw the ball to your cut-off man who should be your shortstop positioned between you and 3rd base. This solution also applies if there is one out.

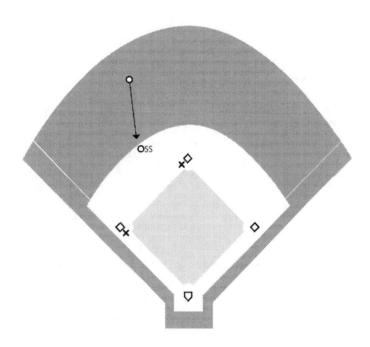

You are the left fielder. The bases are loaded and there are no outs. The ball is grounded to you. Where do you throw the ball?

Answer: The situation here is the same as if there was just a runner on 1st, because the two runners at 2nd and 3rd will score on a base hit. Therefore, your only concern is the 1st base runner that went to 2nd on the hit. To prevent him from going to 3rd, throw to your cut-off man – your shortstop. This solution also applies if there is one out or two outs.

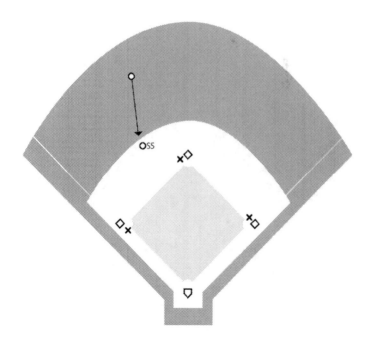

You are the left fielder. The bases are loaded and there are no outs. A fly ball is hit and caught by you. Where do you throw the ball?

Answer: Since the runner at 3rd will tag up and score, your concern is to keep the 2nd base runner from going to 3rd. He would have gone part way and would have gone back to 2nd to tag up. If you throw towards 2nd, the runner may take off for 3rd. You should throw to your cut-off man – the shortstop that should be between you and 3rd base. This solution also applies if there is one out.

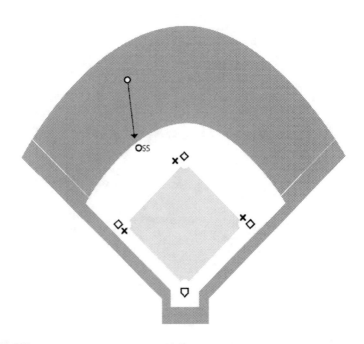

All of the situations for a left fielder can be duplicated for center and right field. The only differences are these. The center fielder's cut-off man can be either the shortstop or the 2nd baseman depending upon which side of 2nd base the ball is hit. The right fielder's cut-off man will be the second baseman.

Due to the arm throwing capabilities of the age of these players this book is addressing, throwing all the way home from an outfield position is not covered.

BASICS OF POSITIONAL BASEBALL WITHOUT THE BALL

Now that the young ballplayer has learned what to do with the ball once it is hit to him, what about where he positions himself when the ball goes to another player. This thinking element of the game is next important because he may end up being involved in the play. Besides thinking "where do I throw the ball if it is hit to me", he also must think "where do I go if the ball is not hit to me". In this area we will outline some basic positioning by infielder with a few outfield situations. This knowledge coupled with the throwing situations will give the ballplayer total smarts when it comes to situation baseball.

FIRST BASEMAN

1ˢᵗ – 1

You are the 1ˢᵗ baseman. There is a runner on 1ˢᵗ and there is one out. The ball is hit to right field as a single. As the batter rounds 1ˢᵗ base, where should you be?

Answer: The throw will come from the right fielder to the second baseman who has gone out to be the relay or cut off man. He will then look to see if either runner has over run the base. You should be on 1ˢᵗ base to receive a throw.

1ˢᵗ – 2

You are the 1ˢᵗ baseman. There is a runner on 2ⁿᵈ and there are no outs. The ball is singled to right field. Where should you position yourself?

Answer: The 2ⁿᵈ base runner will probably try to score. The second baseman will go out to be the relay man. You should position yourself just inside the 1ˢᵗ to 2ⁿᵈ baseline on a line between the right fielder and home plate. Either the right fielder or the 2ⁿᵈ baseman will throw the ball toward you. If you hear nothing from your catcher, let the ball go to home plate. If you hear "cut" from your catcher, catch the ball and watch the runner at 1ˢᵗ to prevent him from going to 2ⁿᵈ.

1st – 3

You are the 1st baseman. There is a slow runner on 2nd and there is one out. It is in the middle innings and your team is down by a run. The second baseman is playing toward second. The ball is hit to your right. You run and dive deep in the hole but the ball goes into right center field where your right fielder quickly gets the ball and wants to cut the runner down going home. Where do you go?

Answer: Since you are out of position to be the cut off man (which your 3rd baseman now assumes), you should go to 2nd base to take a cut off throw if the batter wants to try to take 2nd on the throw towards the plate. Remember, your 2nd baseman has gone out to be the relay man.

1st – 4

You are the 1st baseman. The bases are empty and there are two outs. The batter hits what looks to be a double and maybe a triple to left center field. The shortstop goes out to be the relay man, but your 2nd baseman goes out to back him up. Where should you go?

Answer: Once you know the batter will take 2nd base, you should follow him to 2nd in case he decides to hold up. If he over runs the bag, someone is there to take the throw. You have no reason to stand at 1st base.

1st – 5

You are the 1st baseman. There is a runner at 2nd and two outs. A single is hit down the 3rd base line. The 2nd base runner will easily score. The left fielder throws to his relay man (the shortstop) who then throws to 2nd trying to get the runner who has overrun 2nd base. Where do you go during this play?

Answer: You should position yourself about twenty feet behind second base and in line with the throw coming from the shortstop to catch any errant throw or a loose ball.

Basically, once the batter is committed to going to 2nd base, the 1st baseman's responsibility for staying with 1st base is over. He is then to serve as a cut off man or a backup on throws.

SECOND BASEMAN

2nd – 1

You are the 2nd baseman. There is a runner on 1st and 2nd and there is one out. There is a deep pop up behind 1st base. The right fielder doesn't look like he will get to the ball, but maybe the 1st baseman will. Where do you go?

Answer: You should go to 1st base. The runner will have gone part way to 2nd to make it if the ball drops in for a hit, or he must get back to 1st if it is caught. Your shortstop will cover 2nd for you.

2nd – 2

You are the 2nd baseman. There is a runner on 3rd and there are two outs. There is a bunt down the 1st base line. Where do you go?

Answer: You must head for 1st base. The 1st baseman will most certainly head for the bunt as will the pitcher. You will need to take the throw to end the inning. If the 1st baseman stays and lets the pitcher field the ball, you will need to back up the throw to 1st.

2nd – 3

You are the 2nd baseman. There is a runner on 1st and there is one out. A line drive single is hit to right field. Where do you go?

Answer: On all balls hit to right field or right center field, you are the relay or cut off man. Go part way into right field to pick up the throw and relay it to another position, in this case to 2nd base. If the right fielder is close enough he may want to throw to second in which case you will be the guide. Stand in the line of the throw with your arms in the air as if signaling a touchdown. If the shortstop calls "cut", you can catch the ball, turn and run the ball into the infield. In this situation you will want to check the runner that has gone to third.

2nd – 4

You are the 2nd baseman. It is the bottom of a late inning with runners on 1st and 2nd and there are two outs and your team is up by one run. The pitcher throws a ball into the dirt that gets away from the catcher to his right. The 2nd base runner makes a bee line to 3rd, but the 1st base runner hesitates and then starts for 2nd. The catcher throws the ball to you covering 2nd. The base runner stops – you now have him in a run down. However, the runner that went to 3rd is standing part way down the line towards home. Do you continue the run down or throw to home to prevent a tied game?

Answer: If you can tag the runner without a two toss or more run down before the run scores, you are out of the inning. This would be your first choice. If you tag the runner out after the runner scores, the inning is over, but the run counts.

$2^{nd} - 5$

You are the second baseman. There is a runner at 1st and there is one out. A single is hit to left field. Where do you go?

Answer: On all balls hit to left or left center field you are responsible for covering 2nd base. In this situation your shortstop goes out to relay the throw.

SHORTSTOP

SS – 1

You are the shortstop. There is a runner on 1st and there is one out. A single is hit to right field. Where do you go?

Answer: Your second baseman will go out to be the relay man, so you go to cover 2nd base. You need to tell the second baseman to "cut" the throw if the runner is not coming to 2nd. On a deep single, the second baseman is going to relay the throw to you to prevent the batter from going to 2nd or he will throw to the first baseman acting as a cutoff man in case the now 3rd base runner wants to try and score.

SS – 2

You are the shortstop. There are runners at 1st and 3rd and one out. The batter swings and hits a little dribbler down the first base line. The 1st baseman and the pitcher go for the ball. Where do you go?

Answer: Since 1st base was vacated, the second baseman has to go to 1st to cover, leaving 2nd base open which is where you go. The runner on 3rd will likely score, so whoever fields the ball may want to cut down the lead runner by throwing to you.

SS – 3

You are the shortstop. There is a runner at 1st and 2nd and one out. The ball is bunted down the 3rd base line. Where do you go?

Answer: You must go to cover 3rd since your 3rd baseman would have gone in to field the bunt. It is very likely the throw will come to 3rd to cut down the lead runner. Even without a man on 2nd, you need to cover 3rd in case any runner tries to advance on an errant throw.

SS – 4

You are the shortstop. There is a runner on 1st and there is one out. A single is hit to left field. Where do you go?

Answer: You are to go into short left field. Since the runner from 1st will reach 2nd, the left fielder should throw the ball to you as the relay man. You can come straight out to receive the throw therefore you are in a position to see both 2nd and 3rd. You want to keep the runner from advancing to 3rd base.

You are the shortstop. There is a runner at first and there are two outs. Your team is up by two runs and it is late in the game. A single is hit into left field but to the left fielder's right a little down the line. Since it is taking more time to get to the ball the 1st base runner will be thinking of going to 3rd as he rounds the bag at 2nd. Where do you position yourself?

Answer: Instead of going straight out into left field, you now must position yourself between the left fielder and 3rd base. The left fielder now has the option of throwing to you as a relay to 3rd base or using you as a guide for his throw. Hold your arms in the air as if signaling a football touchdown and listen for your 3rd baseman to call "cut". If you cut off the throw, you still may need to throw to 3rd or to 2nd depending upon where the runner is.

Helpful hint: If you had lined up between the left fielder and 2nd base which tells your left fielder to aim the throw towards 2nd, as soon as the he releases the ball, the 2nd base runner who has rounded the bag and has a "lead off" from 2nd will head toward 3rd. What has happened is the throw was "behind" the runner. You normally always want to throw to the base that is ahead of the runner.

SS – 6

You are the shortstop. The bases are loaded and there is one out. Your team is down by one run and the game is in the middle innings. A sharp line single is hit straight to the left fielder. The coach has instructed your team to go home with any throw. Where do you go?

Answer: The left fielder is going to throw home. The pitcher will go to back up the catcher and the 3rd baseman will be the cut off man standing a third of the way to the plate. You need to go and cover 3rd base in case the catcher or pitcher throws to 3rd after a play at the plate or the 3rd baseman cuts the throw and wants to get the 1st base runner who has decided to try to make it to 3rd.

SS – 7

You are the shortstop. There is a runner on 2nd base and there are no outs. The ball is hit to the 3rd baseman's left and to your right. You both go for the ball, but the 3rd baseman cuts it off and throws to 1st. Where should you go?

Answer: Since 3rd base is open and the 2nd base runner can advance on the throw, you should continue toward 3rd to cover that base for a throw from your 1st baseman.

THIRD BASE

$3^{rd} - 1$

You are the third baseman. There is a runner at 1st and there is one out. A single is sliced down the first base line into right field. The 1st base runner stumbles on his way to second. The 2nd baseman has gone out to relay the throw, but the right fielder decides to throw all the way to 2nd base on his own where your shortstop is covering. Where should you be?

Answer: You should position yourself about twenty feet behind 2nd base in line of the throw for an over throw or if it gets through your shortstop. If the runner tries to go to 3rd, your pitcher should be there to take a throw.

$3^{rd} - 2$

You are the 3rd baseman. The bases are loaded and there is one out. Your team is ahead by three runs and it is late into the game. Your coach has instructed the team to prevent as many runs as possible which means all throws are coming to home plate. The ball is lined as a hit into left center where your center fielder who was playing in a little fields the ball and wants to throw home. Where should you be positioned?

Answer: Put yourself just to the side of the pitcher's mound on the 3rd base side. The pitcher has gone to

144

home to back up the catcher and the shortstop went to cover 3rd. You are now the cut off man in case the catcher wants you to cut the throw from the center fielder and throw to another base.

$3^{rd} - 3$

You are the 3rd baseman. There is a runner on 3rd and there is one out. The batter checks his swing but hits a little blooper a few feet down the 1st base line. The pitcher and the catcher both think they can catch it in the air but it drops. Where should you be going?

Answer: With a man on 3rd, the catcher should not be moving far from home plate. As soon as you see him move away from the plate, you need to go to home plate to cover for a throw if the 3rd base runner goes. Your shortstop will come over to cover 3rd.

$3^{rd} - 4$

You are the 3rd baseman. There are runners at 2nd and 3rd and no outs. The batter hits a pop up into foul territory half way down the 1st base line. The catcher has gone down the line, calls off the 1st baseman, but has to dive and catches the ball. The observant 3rd base runner tags and heads for home where your pitcher has smartly gone to cover. Where should you be?

Answer: You should position yourself about ten feet behind the pitcher in line with the throw coming from your catcher to back up an errant throw. If the ball gets through the pitcher, look to 3rd where your shortstop is covering for the 2nd base runner who probably tagged up also.

3rd – 5

You are the 3rd baseman. There are runners at 1st and 2nd and there is one out. It is late in the game and the score is tied. A two hopper is hit to your shortstop's right which he snags. Where do you go?

Answer: Don't assume your shortstop will go for a double play starting at 2nd base. You go to 3rd to take the force out throw then look to 2nd for the possibility of the 3rd out.

PITCHER

Pit – 1

You are the pitcher. There is a runner on 2nd and there is one out. The ball is singled into short right field. Where should you go?

Answer: Anytime there is a runner on 2nd or 3rd and the ball is hit to the outfield as a hit, you must move to back up the catcher. For sure the 3rd base runner scores, but your concern will be the 2nd base runner who has a good chance of scoring also.

Pit – 2

You are the pitcher. There is a runner on 1st base and there is one out. The ball is singled into right field. Where should you go?

Answer: You should go to a position to back up 3rd base. The 1st base runner will be looking to round 2nd and go to 3rd and if the throw gets through the 3rd baseman, you can keep that runner from scoring.

Pit – 3

You are the pitcher. There are runners on 1st and 3rd and there are two outs. The ball is hit in the hole between 1st and 2nd but your 2nd baseman makes a diving stop. Where should you be?

Answer: You need to be on your way to 1st base to take the throw because your 1st baseman has been pulled away from the bag. The general rule here is that ANY time the ball is hit to the 1st base side of the infield, the pitcher automatically heads for 1st base. You may get the throw from the 1st baseman, the 2nd baseman, or even the shortstop if the throw went to 2nd base first and is relayed to you for a double play.

Pit – 4

You are the pitcher. There is a runner at 3rd and there are no outs. Your pitch gets past the catcher. Where do you go?

Answer: On any passed ball where runners are in scoring position, your responsibility to cover home plate. This is a very obvious solution – just testing to see if you are awake.

Pit – 5

You are the pitcher. There is a runner at 3rd. The ball is popped up into fowl territory down the 3rd base line. The 3rd baseman was playing deep and the infield was swung around to the right because the batter was left handed. The catcher calls you off the catch. Where should you go?

Answer: Home plate. With no one covering home, the 3rd base runner could easily score on a tag up.

THE OUTFIELD

When a ball is not hit to an outfielder, they still have some responsibility to move to another position on the field. Here is the general outline for each fielder.

Left fielder – The left fielder should back up any throw that comes from the catcher to 3rd base. This could occur if the 3rd base runner bluffed a steal of home. Or the throw could come from a pitcher who was backing up a play at the plate and a runner rounding 2nd base tried to get to 3rd base.

The left fielder should back up any throw coming from the right side of the field to 2nd base. This throw could come from the 1st or 2nd baseman or even the right fielder trying to throw a runner out at 2nd. Some throws can get past even two players covering 2nd base.

The left fielder should back up any throw coming to 3rd base from the right side of the infield. Although he will not have enough time to get into a line of throw say coming from the shortstop, an overthrow can bounce off the fence toward left field and if he has made it to the fowl line and thirty feet beyond 3rd base, he is still in a position for a throw to the plate or to 2nd base.

Center fielder – The center fielder should back up any throw coming to 2nd base from the catcher (attempted steal), or any throw coming to 2nd base from the pitcher or 1st baseman from balls fielded to the right side of the infield. Whether the shortstop or the 2nd baseman is backing up each other, the center fielder simply needs to back up any throw coming to 2nd base.

The center fielder is in a variable position that depending upon whether he plays left or right of center, he will have to share the back up responsibilities on throws to 2nd base with the left and right fielder. Communication here is the key.

Right fielder – The right fielder should back up any throw coming to 2nd base from the left side of the infield. This throw could come from the 3rd baseman or the shortstop trying to throw a runner out at 2nd base. Where the 2nd baseman may have the shortstop to back him up on a throw coming from the 1st baseman, the 2nd baseman will not have the shortstop backing him up from a throw coming from the 3rd baseman.

The right fielder should back up any throw coming to 1st base from the left side of the infield. Although he will not have enough time to get into a line of throw say coming from the shortstop, an overthrow can bounce off the fence toward right field and if he has made it to the fowl line and thirty feet beyond 1st base, he is still in a position to keep the runner from advancing to 3rd base.

The right fielder also must be aware of throws made by the catcher to 1st base. This applies only when the 1st base runner has ventured too far off 1st base after a pitch or a caught fowl ball in the home plate area.

I hope you have enjoyed this book for its usefulness in developing the ballplayer into a smarter and more knowledgeable understanding of the game of baseball. In sports the difference between an average player and a good player can be that one small ingredient of "sense". You hear the terms "hockey sense" or "court smart" or "he's a savvy player". Although the physical ability counts greatly, it's the mental ability of knowing where and when that makes the difference.

NOTES

NOTES

I am a baseball enthusiast with a passion for the sport and an appreciation for the tradition of the great American pastime. I've played baseball from Little League through high school at many positions and learned the game from coaches, dad, books, and movies. Visiting the Baseball Hall of Fame in Cooperstown, PA. was very inspiring and instilled the deep passion for a sport created in this great country and what it represents about our competitive values.

In attending my grandsons' baseball games, it has always perplexed me as to why many youngsters are simply confused with what to do with the ball after fielding it. Many of the dad coaches try to instruct this as they go in game situations. The practice time is filled with how to field a grounder, how to catch a fly ball, how to run, how to throw, how to bat, all of which is definitely needed. But we must add the "smarts" to the game. Knowing what the player should do with the ball BEFORE it is hit, makes for a fully developed ballplayer.

My wife and I live in the medium size Midwestern town of Columbus, Indiana. Although born and raised here, I've spent most of my career in Missouri, Michigan and Indiana. Recently moving back to my hometown to semi-retire has allowed me more time to attend yet more youth baseball games which this community has developed into several city and county leagues utilizing 27 ball fields. We are blessed with fine facilities hosting many nationally recognized tournaments.